On the Way to Omega…

(How I accidentally got reborn and heard the voice of God)

June Anne Abele

Copyright © 2017 June Anne Abele

All rights reserved.

ISBN: 9781973241393

Scripture quotations taken from the Amplified® Bible (AMPC), Copyright © 1954, 1958, 1962, 1964, 1965, 1987 by The Lockman Foundation Used by permission. www.Lockman.org" unless otherwise noted.

Cover Photo by Matt Nelson on https://unsplash.com/ used by permission

'Sing A New Psalm...' and 'Thorn In My Pride', written by June Anne Abele, on TheLord'sPoetree.com used by permission

Any brand names or titles have been used to describe factual situations and therefore no compensation was given or received for their use in this book, but they are appreciated by the author.

DEDICATION

This book was written for those who need hope and the unconditional love of God...

CONTENTS

	Acknowledgments	vi
1	A Mini History Lesson	1
2	Stunted Growth	16
3	Wandering in My Own Private Desert	31
4	Exodus for a Party of One	56
5	Accidentally Getting Born Again	74
6	Dreams vs. Visions & "Who is that Dude?"	91
7	He Meets You Where You Are	118
8	Denomination & Obligations vs. Galatians	143
9	Communion, 3rd Day Vision & Healing	169
10	Testing, Testing, One, Two, Three	189
11	Parting, Pruning, Promises & the Platypus	222
12	The Lord's Poetree in Motion...	249
13	No Coincidences & No Degree of separation	269
14	Uncommon Blessing & Final Exam	290
	Poems	311

ACKNOWLEDGMENTS

Thanks be

To God the Father, God the Son and God the Holy Spirit…Joyfully I am yours and You are mine…

Thanks also

To my family, friends and neighbors mentioned in this book and to those who are in my heart.

Thanks lastly

But not at all least-ly, to those who bought any format of this book, because you are now part of any good that comes from it and I count you as a blessing.

If you stole a copy of this book, well then, if you share it with someone I will consider that a form of payment and I forgive you. :)

1- A MINI HISTORY LESSON

And to this people you shall say, Thus said the LORD: Behold, I set before you the way of life and the way of death. Jeremiah 21:8 (AMPC)

Several years ago toward the end of summer I woke up in the middle of the night, at 3:00 am to be exact. I decided to go out onto the front deck of my home. These days I live in Upstate, NY, on top of a mountain in a small house, with only a few neighboring farms strewn down the road. There is a wonderfully clear view of the sky and some distant mountains. This particular night was warm, with a barely-there cool breeze and a slight haze forming across a full moon. The crickets were chirping in rhythm and there was a dreamlike quality to the night.

As I looked upward, I saw the brightness of the hazy moon encircled and glowing with colored rings of silver, gold and orange. So spectacular, It looked to me like God's watchful eye keeping guard over the night with surreal quietness. I felt such a sense of peace in that moment, that I spoke my thanks to Him right out loud, for providing such a wondrous night sky and this peaceful little niche on the mountain. It was like two old friends having a comfortable conversation, just hanging out somewhere in the night. After a while, I took one more deep breath of the sweet night air, I said goodnight and went back inside to bed.

As I woke later that morning I had a vision... there was a large piece of cardboard or poster board with *"June 1:16"* written in black marker, over and over again in various shapes and sizes and then the vision faded.

I thought, OK, this is some kind of message for me. I had recently used markers and cardboard for a church event poster, June is my name, but what is 1:16? It wasn't the time of day, so I figured it must be a chapter and verse in the Bible, but which part? I'd read through the Bible, but was certainly no expert, or someone who could memorize and quote chapter and verse. Did I miss a word in those few seconds? Maybe it didn't say June, or maybe it also said John! I got my Bible and flipped through and found, *I John*, but it only went to verse, 1:10. I looked in, *II John*, but it only went to 1:13, and *III John* only went to 1:14. After flipping through a few more chapters with no success and being frustrated at randomly searching, I decided to start at the beginning with the appropriately titled **Book of Genesis** and proceed from there. A-Ha! There it was!

And God made the two great lights; the greater light to rule the day, and the lesser light to rule the night: He made the stars also. Genesis 1:16 (AMPC)

Chills ran through my body. "How cool is that?" I thought. He heard me, He was with me, He replied...to me! Little ol' me...A mere spec in the universe and He took the time to amaze me, give me the chills and make me smile from ear to ear. He probably had a chuckle at my search method, which happens pretty much every time He speaks to me or sends a message. I am not always sure at first if I received the whole message, or interpreted it correctly. Hearing from the Lord seems to be on a need to know basis, even when I think I need to know more. However on that very basis, I found the Bible is the best reference manual for a relationship with God, or any other relationship. It is *the* book to live by and that is perhaps the built-in-intention of His message.

But He replied, It has been written, Man shall not live and be upheld and sustained by bread alone, but by

every word that comes forth, from the mouth of God.
Matthew 4:4 (AMPC)

This was not the only time the Lord spoke to me through a written mental image. I actually prayed that He might do this sometimes, as a way for me to remember certain things He wanted me to know. It's like taking a photo or a screen-shot in my mind. Other times He speaks His messages in words that I can hear or through dream-like visions. There are many other ways He uses to reach us, letting us know He is right here with us...always. Each and every time I am thrilled and yes, amazed, at how He confirms His faithful presence in my life and the lives of my family, friends and neighbors. I am extremely grateful that He did not give up on me, until I finally understood; we can have a relationship with God the father, through Jesus Christ, and actually hear His voice through the Holy Spirit, who is our guide and teacher.

Nowadays I have what I refer to as a rolling conversation with God throughout my day, in which I do most of the talking and He chimes in whenever He decides I need to hear something. It's a wireless connection without taxes and fees!

This wasn't always the case. There came a point in my life where I nearly missed out on this precious relationship by trying to end my life, and I shudder to think where I might have spent eternity. Part of God's plan is for us to let go of the past and come up higher, so part of my past is written here as my testimony of how God's love changes a messed life into a blessed life filled with joy and hope.

For now, before I get to where I'm going to be for all eternity, let me give you a glimpse of my beginning here on earth around the early 1960's.

Whatever decade you were born in is only one of the factors that contribute to who you will become or what you accomplish in life. Pretty much everything you come in contact with while you're growing up can influence the direction you travel during your finite earthly journey. Even if your intention is to boogie on down life's road living a clean and simple life, you should be aware that evil most assuredly exists to provide you with detours. They come like subtle curves in the road but lead to parts unknown. There's an alternate route, an unexpected delay, or an extended vacation at an oasis that turns out to be a mirage in the desert and before you know it you're in a car with *Thelma and Louise* about to go over a cliff.

I did that. I went over the cliff... and in mid air... I was rescued.

Being born into a Catholic family, however dysfunctional it was at the time, my two sisters and I did what all Catholic kids were supposed to do. We were born and Baptized, received Holy Communion, and Confirmation. We learned about the Sacraments and Bible stories at church service or Sunday school. In addition, there was Wednesday afternoon Bible study if you went to public school back in those days.

I liked to go to church when I was young; I loved learning about God and Jesus, although they didn't really teach much about the Holy Spirit, whom they referred to then as the Holy Ghost. We had those classic pictures of Jesus on our bedroom walls, where He was surrounded by happy children, Cherubs and lambs, sitting on a rock near streams of water...all aglow with streaming sunlight! I had my very own kid's Bible. I watched movies like, *The Song of Bernadette* or *Lilies of the Field, The Trouble With Angels* and *Where Angels Go Trouble Follows*. As a child I took all that religious stuff pretty seriously because it made me feel special to be a part of it.

Somewhere in that learning process around the age of five or six, I stood in the living room of our house with my two sisters, having a kid's conversation about God and the devil. My older sister informed us how God is great and good and he loves us, but the devil is always chasing us and trying to get us before we can get to see God in Heaven. To a kid, being chased by the devil can be a pretty scary thing. At times, so was my older sister. So I boldly declared, right then and there, "The devil can never catch me because I already love God and I started before now all the way to infinity!" And I said it really, really, fast, so for sure I had a head start in front of that devil.

Infinity was a word my dad had just taught me in describing how the sky goes on forever. I liked that word. Well let me tell you, I don't think the devil liked that word and he must have been listening to our conversation, because shortly afterward the devil showed up in my mouth.

Sometimes my older sister was in charge of us and took me and my younger sister to the park to play. That's a lot of power and responsibility to give a kid who was around seven years of age. I wanted to play in the giant sandbox, but for some reason my bossy sister would not let me near it. I think she wanted to play hopscotch. I was mad at her, so I screamed the "F" word at the top of my lungs about 20 times in a row. It was another word I had recently learned. Although I did not know its meaning, I did know it was a bad word. So did all the people in the park who were glaringly staring at me and I remember crying on the way home.

Like any good sister in charge would do, she told my mom what I said. When confronted, I told the truth and my mom marched me down to the basement where she shoved the ever popular bar of Ivory soap into my mouth and washed out the bad words. For sure the bad words must have come out along with my puke on the floor, which I then had to clean. At least I had the Ivory soap to use for the cleanup. This particular soap was advertised in those days as the only pure bar of soap that floats on the water. Sort of like *Jesus*, disguised as a bar of soap! Jesus came disguised as many people, places and things in my life. He left evidence of His presence there for me to find years later. I didn't know then to look for Him, so I didn't see the signs He was with me all that time. I've been blessed with a pretty good memory, probably just so I can share my testimony with you today.

However we grow up, either raised by our parents or lack there of, will be what seems normal for us. We don't know different, so we don't know better...or worse. For all intents and purposes, I think I was a happy child in spite of some very unhappy events.

As I mentioned earlier, my family was what we nowadays call dysfunctional.

In those days growing up in Queens, NY, everything was family oriented, divorce was a rare thing and frowned upon, and most children were disciplined, respectful and educated. For a divorced parent there was not much in the way of resources, support, or reassuring comfort to keep you going forward, even though that is exactly what the church *should* be for people.

My parents were divorced when I was four years old, with my mom having custody of me and my two sisters. My dad was a very smart, witty, likeable guy, especially to his friends and co-workers. He had many, many talents, was organized and efficient, but he was also controlling, an alcoholic and had a violent temper. I am not really sure how far back this behavior went in our family. I remember his father; my grandfather was a likable but very stern man, though I don't recall him abusing alcohol. My father's relationship with his older sister was at times strained from what I remember, but when she moved her family out of state the distance helped keep the peace between them. His younger sister had some form of mental retardation and he set her up in an apartment and took care of her bills, but sometimes he would be very harsh with her and made her cry. His motto was "I'm not always right, but I'm never wrong!"

What may have contributed to my father's alcohol addiction and sudden rages was the loss of my parents' first child, a baby boy who died during childbirth. My father always wanted a son, but eventually wound up with three girls, and I think he somehow blamed my mother for these things for a very long time.

When I was born, my mother sent my baby picture to him because he was overseas. He wrote, "She's too ugly", and sent it back. Gee, thanks Dad, it was a pleasure to meet you too! Oddly enough, sometime after my original birth announcement from the hospital was sent out, my dad decided it wasn't good enough, made a die cast printing block and printed new announcements. He was working for *Everest Records* at the time, so it pictured Mt. Everest, reels of recording tape with the words "Have You Heard the Latest?" I thought that was a pretty cool thing to do and I've kept that block all these years.

We never knew when his mood would change. He had attempted to kill my mom on more than one occasion, including while my mom was pregnant with my older sister. To me it seems unbelievable, that an unborn child could survive such an ordeal through the fear my mom must have felt as it happened. On that occasion he chased her through the house yelling "I'm going to kill you". He came at her with a knife and as she tried to grab it away, he slit her fingers down to the bone. A sweet older couple, who lived downstairs in an apartment of our house, came to her aid, by eventually talking him into giving up the knife and calming him down. Margie & Jimmy Rose were two angels in the night that came to rescue my mom. I wasn't even born yet, but I will never forget their names, nor will the Lord.

And the King will reply to them, Truly I tell you, in so far as you did it for one of the least [in the estimation of men] of these My brethren, you did it for Me.
Matthew 25:40 (AMPC)

My dad was arrested several times for similar behavior, but each time he was eventually released or the charges dropped. There is a bit of politics behind that but I won't go into details. Around the time of their divorce, one of the things I remember was my mom coming back from the hospital with her head covered with a white helmet of gauze bandages. My dad had cracked open my mothers skull on the corner of the doorway and I was standing right there when it happened. Thankfully I do not remember that part. I am sure the Lord in His mercy had spared me from remembering the bloody sight which would have made it almost impossible for me to forgive my dad later in my life.

If you are wondering why the Lord didn't spare my mom this horrible event, then I mention again, although my dad attacked her on more than one occasion, she survived and persevered. The Lord will not let us bear more than we can handle. If my mom had ever learned who she was in Christ, and what help and power was available to her, I believe things would have been different.

Our church was more in the habit of spouting rules which claimed who was not worthy, rather than put the focus where it belongs, which is our individual relationship with Jesus Christ. In any case her life was spared and someone was there to intervene and get help. She got through it and was made stronger to face whatever would come her way in the future.

However in the meantime, it did understandably affect how she handled things which *were* under her control, namely us kids.

My sisters and I are all different. We do have some similarities in our characters which are apparent even now that we are older, but we look different, we act different and we handle the same issues differently. Memories of our childhood together vary, because we were treated differently by our parents and our ages spanned almost four years. When dad was around, we were a lot quieter and sometimes almost afraid to speak. All he had to do was call me over to him and I started to cry because I was afraid of him and most likely he was going to hurt me, even if he was kidding around. Then it was always, " if you don't stop crying, I'll give you something to cry about!" I guess he thought I was faking it and I don't know about you but I was not able to stop crying on demand. I did love him and I tried to obey him, but my obedience was out of fear and not out of love.

Every now and then we would go with him somewhere to visit a relative or friend. He had a lot of friends, some of them wealthy and even famous, because dad was a sound engineer for movies, commercials and music. He eventually remarried and moved to Long Island, so we didn't see him much and maybe that was a good thing. We always seemed to be misbehaving and getting punished because our dad had *lots* of rules.

Even when he wasn't around we still always seemed to be in trouble and constantly battling with each other, always fighting for control inasmuch as we were just kids trying to deal with adult issues. Surely though, we had fun and things were not always as bad as it might sound. After all, we didn't know it should be different and we still loved our parents the best we could with what little understanding we had of the subject.

It was a time when kids could be disciplined by way of getting spanked, smacked, yelled at, slapped, hit with a wooden spoon or belt, washing a dirty mouth out with soap or other fabulous forms of punishment, to suite their particular kiddie-crimes. I had even gone to school with welts on my face in the shape of my mom's hand. She cried when she saw what she did. I cried from the pain and for whatever I did to make her so mad.

Sometimes even when we weren't misbehaving, there was still disciplinary actions called chores. Although learning these skills were a benefit to us later in life, in my opinion it was a bit too severe for children of our age to handle as much as we did. One sister was a year and a half older and the other, two years younger than me. We took turns doing dishes, laundry, shopping, washing floors, pet care, vacuuming, dusting, ironing, sewing, cooking, etc... I learned to do all these things before age nine. My older sister got the harder tasks and so on down the line she would teach me and my younger sister. I remember my younger sister looking like a tiny waif, around age four or five, needing a chair to stand on just to reach the sink faucets and wash the dishes.

Our mom never learned to drive, most likely because my dad was the one trying to teach her, so we walked to all the neighborhood stores. Malls or mega department stores did not exist yet where we lived, so we had separate dry goods, grocery, and delicatessen and butcher stores. Mom would make the shopping list and send us out together to bring back what we needed in brown paper bags. This was also before the invention of plastic bags with handles or reusable shopping bags. Even in winter, my younger sister and I would hold the bags of groceries while my older sister pulled us all the way home on a sled.

Being divorced, with my dad rarely ever paying child support and never paying alimony, my mom had to find work that could support us all. She had some decent business skills and a good friend was able to set up a make-shift office in our basement so they could work as key-punch operators. Key punch operators were the old-school computer data entry people, who keyed in letters, which punched holes through corresponding pre-numbered stock cards that a computer could then read. It was very tedious work, but at least she could be at home as she could not afford to pay a babysitter.

Our mom worked hard and she worked long hours

which left her very tired and left us kids to do the chores that parents usually do.

With school, chores and homework, there wasn't much time left for fun or to go to church, and my mother being divorced, was what they called,

excommunicated-

(officially exclude (someone) from participation in the sacraments and services of the Christian Church).

Doesn't that seem like the church divorced her for being divorced?

Sometimes she would send us to church with our Nana and Pop-Pop, (grandparents) who lived nearby. A couple of years later my Nana and Pop-Pop moved to Bayridge, Brooklyn, so I only got to church on holidays or when I stayed with them during the summer. As far as my mom knew, she was no longer welcomed to go to church and receive Holy Communion. She must have felt unjustly abandoned and unloved by God, although to the best of her ability as we grew, she made sacrifices for us to keep going to church and put money in the collection plate.

To me it didn't seem right that they could kick you out of church or find fault because you divorced someone who tried to kill you.

2- STUNTED GROWTH

All of you must keep awake (give strict attention, be cautious and active) and watch and pray, that you may not come into temptation. The spirit indeed is willing, but the flesh is weak. Matthew 26:41   Amplified Bible, Classic Edition (AMPC)

When I was nine years old, my mom was able to move us into a slightly nicer house and neighborhood. Several blocks away there was a nice Catholic church next door to a Catholic grade school. By this time my mom was making enough money to be able to send two out of the three of us to Catholic school. There wasn't an opening for my grade at that time since it was mid-year, so I went to the local public school. Mom said maybe I could go to Catholic school next year but it never happened.

Like anything else in life there are pluses and minuses to any school. I did want to go to Catholic school, but I really liked my public school and had some really great teachers, who I remember to this day as having an impact on my life. One in particular, was my English teacher Ms. Piderit, who I also had for homeroom each day before classes started. Ms. Piderit, both inside and out was naturally beautiful. She looked like a model, tall, slim, long flowing hair, with a beautiful clear complexion. But it wasn't her outward appearance that captivated me so much as it was her mannerisms and calming presence as she spoke and taught us more than just English. She had poise, patience and was never harsh or crass with the students, which are qualities not every teacher displays in a room of anxious pre-teen students.

I loved that she used modern music and poetry examples in her lessons because both music and poetry always held my interest. She showed connections from lyrics or poems to our own everyday lives and experiences.

It was the 1970's at an assembly, when Ms. Piderit read an article from the morning newspaper, which described a terrible accident that happened to a mother and child on a train. The child walked between the two train cars and fell through as the mother tried to grab hold but could not and the child was killed. We had a moment of silent prayer (which was allowed in those days) and then she played Paul Simon's, Mother & Child Reunion. It was something that touched my heart and soul.

Another time in class, she used the Judy Collins version of the song "Both Sides Now" as an example of seeing things from another point of view. Our assignment was to write of a similar experience from our own life. I asked if I could write it as another verse of the song and she said that was a great idea. I turned in my work and the next day on my way to class I saw a big poster on display in the hallway with my words and my name on it. I was very surprised and it felt weird to see it there, but she told me she thought I had potential to be a good writer. No one had ever encouraged me that way before.

In those days it was very common that kids were reading at least two to three years beyond their grade level. The particular school I attended happened to be an experimental school of sorts and was classified as an intermediate school for a specific period of years. So it was a P.S.I.S. only for those exact years I attended, which meant that I had Ms. Piderit as one of my teachers for an additional two years before I went to high school. In that time we had some good conversations about family, life, dreams, and she became sort of a role model for me.

One time she even drove me home after school because

it was raining and it was on her way home. When we got to my house she told me her sister was also a teacher in a school not far from my house...a Catholic school. It turned out that her sister was a Sister, a nun who was teaching in my sister's school! So this might sound like a coincidence but to me it seemed that no matter where I wound up going to school, I was supposed to have a Ms. Piderit in my life and I count that as a blessing.

I was a kid who actually liked school. Not the homework so much, but just being in school learning new things. English, Social Studies and Science were my favorite subjects. I earned decent grades without much trouble. Since this was an experimental intermediate school, I was able to choose alternative subjects like they do in high school and college. I chose Law Studies and Occult Studies.

Law Studies was fascinating to me, sort of an abbreviated first year college course in which we were able to study famous court cases and even went to sit in on civil cases in court.

Occult Studies also fascinated me and came complete with a teacher who looked like Snidely Whiplash, who famously tied down a damsel on the train tracks. (See Snidely Whiplash, image search online). Mr. D'amica was mysterious, tall and dark and had one of those long, crazy twisted mustaches that came to a point sticking out on either side of his face. He was funny and a strangely compelling storyteller which some might have found, maybe a little too creepy. We sat alphabetically so my desk was right up front facing his desk. One time I was so engrossed in the reading assignment that I didn't notice he had been trying to get my attention until he dropped a big stapler loudly on his desk. It caused me to jump and look up to see most of the class laughing along with him. However, he told me he was thrilled that I had such good concentration. I did. I wasn't a slow reader, but I liked to spend extra time rereading passages, as if I were directing the movie in my head as I read, checking the scenery, studying the characters and noting details. We studied authors like Samuel Taylor Coleridge and Daphne DuMaurier, among others. For me it was an intriguing introduction to more sister authors and a journey down a road I wish I had not traveled. It didn't happen all at once, it came sort of like the fog or a fine mist. It slowly envelops you but you can still see…just not as clearly…and you don't need an umbrella for protection…because it's not really raining…and yet…you still get wet. Without also learning spiritual discernment, it can be difficult to understand that not everything we learn in school is true or for our good.

All through grade school and some of high school I still went to church on most Sundays and of course all the obligatory Catholic holidays. My older sister played guitar and sang at the church folk mass, which made it more fun to go to worship, because these songs reflected the praise and hope of a younger generation. It made up for having to hear the monotone voice of the kid chosen to stumble through that weeks reading from the Bible. If you're not familiar with that Church tradition, then picture a shy fourth grader reading the mandatory report of, *what I did on my summer vacation,* on his first day at a new school. There's nervous concerned facial expression but no emotional connection or understanding of the words they're reading; they are *just reporting the facts Ma'am*.

Besides the lack of excitement, week after week I noticed I was always overheated and felt like I might faint. I joked with my friends that maybe I was like *Damien* from the *Omen* movie and the church was making me sick, and in an abstract way it was doing just that.

I did have asthma but it wasn't the cause of feeling faint. I know *now* that I actually had a chronic condition that went undiagnosed for many years. Consequently, I started going to church to pick up the weekly bulletin to show as proof that I went to church, but I just didn't stay for the duration. A lot of my friends did that, so if everyone is doing it, maybe it's just a partial sin?

It's also *possible* my memory is wrong about this, but once or twice I thought about keeping the money from the envelope that I was supposed to put in the collection plate. (If this was an email I would insert a winking smiley face here.)

Oh, I forgot to mention going to confession. According to how the Catholic nuns taught us, we need to go to confession every week and tell the priest all our current sins and promise not to do them anymore. Then the priest would absolve us and tell us how many prayers to say for penance. If we confessed a few minor sins, we might have had to say two *Hail Mary's*. If we had a more sinful week, we might have had to say three *Hail Mary's* and two *Our Fathers*. *Penance* is self-punishment. Our amount of punishment prayers are according to our particular amount of sinfulness. If we skipped a few weeks of confession, we even had to tell that to the priest and he would add it to our list of sins. If you were like me and eventually stopped going to confession or church (except for Christmas & Easter because, after all...that was the Christian thing to do.), then you too probably racked up enough sins that if you wrote them down, you could fill several rolls toilet paper. Then what do we do? According to them, we are not worthy to receive communion. So first my mother and my father are kicked out, and now I've become *waaay* too embarrassed to drag my entire collection of toilet paper rolls into a confessional booth and give the Priest a heart attack. That would surely require extra penance. Could I ever say enough prayers to be forgiven? Would I have enough breath to say 1,000,000 Hail Mary's and Our Father's? I mean, did I mention I had asthma!

But you know.... I was a bit confused.... I still loved God

and I knew He was still up there but, didn't I learn that Jesus died for all my sins? Was He killed **because of us** or was He sacrificed **for us**? It would seem they meant we are all at fault because He was crucified, so we who share in the blame should share in the punishment. But...He was our **once and for all sacrifice**, so severely beaten and then crucified with blood poured out...actually nailed to the cross, **as punishment for all** of our sins...past, present and future. He never sinned...yet He did this **willingly** *for us* and took the punishment that we deserved because of our sins. When something has already been given to us freely from God, it can not be taken away from us and there is no need for additional punishment.

For God so loved the world that He gave His one and only Son, that everyone who believes in Him shall not perish but have eternal life.For God did not send His Son into the world to condemn the world, but to save the world through Him.Whoever believes in Him is not condemned, but whoever does not believe is already condemned, because he has not believed in the name of God's one and only Son   John 3:16-18 (AMPC)

See what I mean? If we are *not condemned by God* because we believe in Jesus, then why is it presented to some of us, as we must *do penance to be forgiven by*

God? It certainly seems like condemnation and partiality, if a church continues to tell people they are unworthy sinners week after week, or does not allow them to partake in the Lord's Supper, which Jesus told us to do in remembrance of Him!

And he took bread, and gave thanks, and broke it, and gave to them, saying, This is my body which is given for you: this do in remembrance of me. Luke 22:19 (AMPC)

Are we forgiven or not? If you are made to feel guilty and condemned, how do you remain hopeful and how are we able to help others know the truth? Who would want to sign up for that kind of life? We all sin and we all need His forgiveness.

If you really fulfill the royal law according to the Scripture, "You shall love your neighbor as yourself," you are doing well. But if you show partiality, you are committing sin and are convicted by the law as transgressors. For whoever keeps the whole law but fails in one point has become guilty of all of it.

 James 2:8-10 (AMPC)

No Christian person can kick their neighbor out of church or keep them from worship or communion without condemning themselves in the process. Really, who among us can cast that first stone? I sure don't know anyone who could...*except* Jesus, and He does not condemn us... he loves us unconditionally, which means we are *already* forgiven because of His sacrifice. And to know that truth sets you free.

For the law of the Spirit of life in Christ Jesus hath made me free from the law of sin and death.   Romans 8:2

Who then is the one who condemns? No one. Christ Jesus who died--more than that, who was raised to life--is at the right hand of God and is also interceding for us.

Who shall separate us from the love of Christ? shall tribulation, or distress, or persecution, or famine, or nakedness, or peril, or sword?   Romans 8:34-35 (AMPC)

The Christian Church, is not supposed to make us feel condemned and unworthy because we sin, but it should remind us to be grateful that we are so blessed and have already been forgiven. We are not supposed to pick and choose which sins are forgivable. We can not disinvite from the table, those who want to worship our Lord and Savior, Jesus Christ who extended the invitation to whomsoever believes.

Let us not therefore judge one another any more: but judge this rather, that no man put a stumbling block or an occasion to fall in his brother's way.   Romans 14:13 (AMPC)

Somewhere along the line The Church broke off into different denominations. A number of them, in attempt to control the flock, decided that if people know they are already forgiven for *all* sins past, present and future that they will see this as an opportunity to freely go around sinning. It's simply not the case and it is prejudgment. Sure there will be exceptions, but it is not for the Church to impose their own will and try to remove the choice which God has freely given.

Imagine something like you're driving your car, talking on your hand held cell phone, or maybe trying to swat that fly with your hand while thinking, *where the heck did that fl...* and **Bang**! You smash into the back of a shiny new BMW...and uh-oh...you just remembered you let your insurance lapse. That guy you just sent to the hospital, can sue you and take everything you own away from you...and he can do it because you my friend are clearly at fault. Instead, this guy turns to you and tells you, I forgive you and I will take care of all the damage, and even give you a new car, because I belive it was not your intention to hurt me. You knew it was your fault, but he let you off the hook. Would you continue to be a careless driver, figuring you got away with it once, why worry about doing it again? Or would you be so grateful to the guy for having taken that heavy burden off of you, and having given you a new car to drive, that you would be not only a more careful driver, but you realize you are even able to forgive that neighbor who dinged your new car the following week.

For you were called to freedom, brethren; only do not turn your freedom into an opportunity for the flesh, but through love serve one another. Galatians 5:13

I should pause right about here because, *I would like to be clear, I am not Church bashing nor am I against any particular denomination of Christianity*. I love God the Father, God the Son and God the Holy Spirit. I love the Christian Church which continues to grow. I also continue to grow by attending service at brick and morter churches regardless of the denomination as long as there are annointed preachers. However I believe in the personal relationship with our Lord and Savior over the rules or regulations of any physical Church. Even if I didn't attend Church, I would still have my personal relationship through Jesus Christ and the Holy Spirit to lead me in God's plan for my life. But I reiterate, I love God, love my Church and love my Bible.

I am only offering my individual perception of growing up in the Christian Church and comprehension of God's Word, through life experiences that are unique to me as I continue to grow in Christ.

And Jesus said to him, Forbid him not: for he that is not against us is for us.   Luke 9:50

While my circumstance and individual relationship with Jesus might be unique, my testimony is like one star in the universe, one of many who were blind but now see and now know *who they are in Christ*. We have one life with a choice to travel either a secular or spiritual road, but we can't divide ourselves to travel both at the same time. I ask only that you consider your own set of circumstances and whether or not you are hearing the *gospel truth* and therefore, are you being blessed and refreshed in your current relationships? Do you wake up and say, "Yippee!... Thank you Lord for this day and please help me to be a blessing to someone today"? If not, then maybe you've lost faith in God, or you're faithfully following rules of the Church, but unaware of the supreme,interactive relationship you can have in and with Jesus Christ. By interactive, I mean that you have to necessarily believe *He* is active and wants you not only to receive the salvation He has already given us, but to hear His voice and be led by the Spirit. God, in His infinate wisdom, mercy and grace even gave us the faith we need to do so, by imprinting His Word upon our hearts and in our minds. Therefore we have the ability to recognize His Word, as truth when we read it or hear it read, and actively be taught or led by the Holy Spirit.

For this is the covenant that I will make with the house of Israel after those days, says the Lord: I will imprint My laws upon their minds, even upon their innermost thoughts and understanding, and engrave them upon their hearts; and I will be their God, and they shall be My people. And it will nevermore be necessary for each one to teach his neighbor and his fellow citizen or each one his brother, saying, Know (perceive, have knowledge of, and get acquainted by experience with) the Lord, for all will know Me, from the smallest to the greatest of them

Hebrews 8:10-11+9 (AMPC)

But the natural, nonspiritual man does not accept or welcome or admit into his heart the gifts and teachings and revelations of the Spirit of God, for they are folly (meaningless nonsense) to him; and he is incapable of knowing them [of progressively recognizing, understanding, and becoming better acquainted with them] because they are spiritually discerned and estimated and appreciated. 1 Corinthians 2:14 (AMPC)

Try not to dismiss as coincidence, the things which may represent a knock at your spiritual door. It may very well be God asking you to pay attention. Listen for the knock, open the door, invite Him in so He can fix what needs fixin'.

Behold, I stand at the door, and knock: if any man hear my voice, and open the door, I will come in to him, and will sup with him, and he with me. Revelation 3:20 (AMPC)

More on that interactive relationship as we move along...

3- WANDERING IN MY OWN PRIVATE DESERT

She was boisterous and rebellious;
She would not stay at home. Proverbs 7:11(AMPC)

I was fourteen years old when I started my freshman year of high school and graduated my senior year at seventeen. During those four years, which were smack-dab in the middle of the 1970's, I was probably just like most teens growing up in that decade, influenced by what's going on in the world and what's going on in my own neighborhood. In school we studied current events. There was the Vietnam War going on, and the protests against it, but it was coming to an end after 20 years. Young people just as in the 1960's still held demonstrations and sit-ins, for peace, freedom and civil rights, but *the times they were a-changin'* and took on a seemingly lighter tone as new things were emerging. With a comedic look at the Korean War, *M.A.S.H.* became a T.V. superstar, *Jesus Christ Superstar* was in theaters, and *Saturday Night Live,* poked no-holds-barred fun at everything on and off the planet, plus they featured a cool musical guest every week and they would play anything from folk to psychedelic funk.

At least that is how things were looking from my corner of the world. I mean there were always worries over terror attacks, serial killers, presidents in turmoil and lions and tigers and bears, oh my! But aside from the big world stuff, I needed that wonderful distraction of comedy and music, because my home life was increasingly stressful.

My mom was not the happy, loving, encouraging sort of mom you might see on the *Happy Days* show. She was raising three girls and working hard to put money in the bank. However, her idea of teamwork or family was to see which of her children had the greatest potential to be of benefit to her. I know she wanted to be happy, I know she loved us, but she had a negative approach to life and complained endlessly about everything. She would complain about our dad, her boyfriends, the neighbors, the people at her job, the people on TV, her children, our friends, what anyone did, what they ate, how they lived, when they did it, how they did it, and what they didn't do. She had two or three good friends, (all coping with their own issues) who actually adored her. However, she lived in fear of inviting them over for dinner or just for company, because to her it seemed our house was never nice enough clean enough or perfect enough that she would not feel embarrassed. She was a self proclaimed perfectionist who knew she was not able to live up to that standard. So instead of focusing on doing the things she could do well, she procrastinated by picking apart everything around her, because as the saying goes, misery loves company.

It is very hard to live with, or even to be around that type of person for any length of time and not have it affect your own behavior one way or the other. You can be repelled into rebellion or unknowingly start to exhibit that very type of behavior you hate to be around, which can infiltrate all of your relationships. I know I did both. I was pretty friendly, usually saw the good side of things, loved meeting all kinds of people and shared whatever I had with them. When I saw sadness or hurting, I wanted to help, and if I saw budding talent, I wanted to be encouraging. I wanted to do something good with my life that would help people, but just didn't know how to get there from where I was. I became rebellious toward my mom, because there was no encouragement for that kind of life or for anything that had meaning for me. Even something as simple as sharing or giving a gift to someone brought accusations of trying to buy friends. I looked at her life and knew that was not who I wanted to be, but sometimes that critical and controlling side of her showed up in me.

When I was a teenager, there was a particular group of friends I would hang around with at a park, which was a couple of miles from my house. New neighbors moved in a few doors down from my house and they had a teenage daughter almost my age. She was pretty, very nice, we got along great and we had fun roaming around the neighborhood just being goofy teens. Eventually I brought her down to meet my "cool" friends at the park. They loved her and she fit right in, so I brought her there more often. One week I was sick with a cold or flu so I didn't go out. I found out afterward that she had gone down to the park all week without me and I was mad. I mean, I was furious and went to her house and yelled at her, for daring to go have fun with MY FRIENDS without me. Those were my friends and I introduced her to them, so it was not fair for her to go behind my back while I was sick, because she never would have met them if it were not for me! I made her cry. Good golly, I was a jerk, yes?

It was sometime later when the incident kept winding up in my thoughts, giving me a very uneasy feeling. I was jittery in the way a person gets when there's something they forgot to do, but can't pinpoint what it is, so it stays in your head. I thought, what's wrong with me… and I thought I heard myself say, "***Why do you want to control her?***" And then I knew… I was doing what was done to me. I was not in any type of behavioral therapy, (though I'm sure my family would have liked that idea) nor had I read any books or magazines on the subject. This little piece of wisdom came from somewhere else...like a voice within, yet I did not know how or why it happened the way it did. It felt like knowing the answers to a test I never studied for, or for that matter, I never knew there was a test. It was indeed the Holy Spirit guiding me but I had no understanding back then.

Now looking back, I know the Holy Spirit was also with me in the second grade, on a particular day in the mid 1960's. I got to school early and sat in the school auditorium waiting for all the new children who would be starting school that day. They called it "bussing". Children from a less fortunate area were bussed into an area where they could receive a better education, which in turn meant there had to be children from our area bussed out somewhere else. Parents were protesting against it and there was a lot of bigotry during that era, and mine was nearly an all white school.

I could just about see the children's heads through the window in the auditorium doors, as they passed by walking down the hall. Then a door swung open and a small black child ran up to me and punched me so hard in my stomach, that I actually lost my breath and gasped for air as he ran back out. I don't know if anyone else even saw what happened. It happened so fast and I just cried, held my stomach and tried to breathe. I remember thinking, "I don't know him, why did he punch me"? Then a thought came into my head, "***He is***

scared to be in this new place". I mean, tears were still rolling down my face when that thought came into my head, but it calmed me down. I understood what happened and I was okay and I was sad for the boy. This wisdom too, surely came courtesy of the Holy Spirit, as well as another time in the fourth grade during lunch break.

I was sitting with a classmate and we were looking through a sixth grader's textbook. She said, "That's too hard for me, I don't understand any of that". I agreed it did look a lot harder than our fourth grade work. Then I told her, "***Don't worry you will be prepared for that work when you get there; we are learning what we need to know for now***". The words came out of my mouth, but I don't know how they got in my head to be able to speak them. It was like I was saying the words out loud and hearing them, while thinking," Well OK then, I feel better now". Why would I have that kind of understanding at the age of nine? It could only be the Holy Spirit, teaching me and comforting me. I certainly was not getting that kind of encouraging wisdom from home. My dad actually protested against children being bussed in and out of our school, and my mom didn't have the patience or understanding herself, that would enable her to help me feel secure or not to worry.

Speaking of home and my mom...

Without a balanced perspective, a daily dose of faith and trust in God to provide what she needed, she put her focus on making money and also looked to us to help provide that security. Instead of uniting her children as a family who works together in harmony, mom pitted us against each other to be in competition for her favor or convoluted idea of love. There was no encouragement or self discovery or even acceptance that we had a choice in the matter, there was only her dictation and direction to be what she felt we should be, and our contribution to her endless *things to do* list.

If I was to come home happy or wanting to share an experience or good news from work, school, or time spent with my friends, it was a matter of minutes before she was able to turn it into something negative and suck the life right out me. If it wasn't about her or for her, it was of no value. Even the matter of buying my sister her first used car turned out to be for the purpose of driving mom around because she never learned to drive, but still it was appreciated. In my mom's defense, it was my dad who tried to teach her and that was scary enough for her to never try to learn again.

This doesn't mean we didn't have love and good times in the family and even hysterical laughter sometimes, but our lives were out of balance.

Like any teen, there are things I wanted to buy which my mom would decide I didn't need, but if I got a job and paid for it myself, she had fewer objections. I began with babysitting, then got my working papers and moved on to delivering circulars, cleaning houses, and eventually at age sixteen, got a job in a local supermarket. We were required to give a portion of our paychecks to mom. Even after high school, for as long as we lived at home, we each had to pay a substantial rent to her. That may have been the case in other families, but not amongst most of my peers, which left me with a feeling of stagnation.

I did pretty well in high school and elected business accounting which came easy to me because bookkeeping was one of my mom's talents, so I was familiar with it and she also felt this should be my career choice. While I was still in high school, my mom had been remarried and divorced again and also we moved two more times. Her relationships with men were probably not based on love but more for convenience and they never lasted very long. Some men were nice enough or bought her a gift now and then and even accepted that she had three young kids. Some were not so nice and stole from her. She mostly wound up with men she could manipulate into doing whatever she wanted them to do and if they did not, there were consequences.

I could see through the years, she had lost any trust she might have had and didn't seem to find security, love, or satisfaction from her relationships. Each time we moved she sold the house for much more than she paid, so money was her security and her way to control that which was out of control in her life.

In the meantime, I was busy going to school, working, and creating my own little world apart from my family. I would spend as much time out of the house as possible without getting kicked out. My sisters were building their own *walls and bridges* and even though we all lived together, it is amazing how distant we were becoming.

I had a lot of friends in school and in the neighborhood. I was not the coolest or the prettiest or the most popular, or the outcast, the wannabe, or the geek, but I did hang out with any and all of those people. I had plenty of insecurities and I was naïve in certain situations, but I liked meeting new people and making friends. I had a genuine interest to listen and to understand people and maybe that's why for the most part they liked me back.

I even managed to make a few life long friends. Yet, I never minded being alone, I liked solitude as much as I like to be around people. If I wasn't with my friends then I was off by myself walking through the streets, or maybe with our dog sitting in the park, writing poetry in my head, or reading books, imagining the world the way it should be instead of how it was. Spiritually I felt a connection with Native Americans, so I liked to read about their beliefs and culture, I was drawn to the simplicity of they way they lived their lives. I also was drawn to the Amish people, who were able to live simply in the modern world. I could see kindness and strength in these groups of people and (being the internet did not exist yet and I was not well traveled) I wondered why the rest of the world as far as I could *see*, didn't seem to want to embrace or understand that kind of living. Greed and self importance came to mind.

At the same time I had a growing interest in reading horror stories and following gruesome crimes in the news. It was like a tug of war in going on for my soul with dreams to match. I always had dreams like any kid would have, such as being chased by someone or looking for a bathroom, only to wake and find out I had to pee! But those teen years and beyond, the dreams were either of a darker nature with shadowy figures, or bright sunny days where I could fly and also teach others to fly. I'll explain more about those dreams later, as they became lucid and more spiritual. I didn't particularly share my dreams with anybody, maybe a few with my sisters or a close friend, but I did spend time studying them on my own, like an observer of my own being. I felt like a loner who enjoyed company.

I also enjoyed music. So much so, that I got a job in a record store while I was in my senior year of high school. That was the same year that Elvis Presley died and I could see for myself by the multitudes of his teary eyed fans, the effect that music can have on a person's life. So when it came time to graduate and start my accounting career, I opted to stay in the music store, where I felt a stronger connection. My mom helped pay for my older sister to go to an art school in NYC, but she didn't see the point to pay for me to go to college or music school. Since I couldn't afford to pay rent and school tuition on my own, I tried to also work part time at my mother's office, but I knew I was not going to be happy within those walls no matter what the salary would be there. She was not approving of my choice to stay in the record store, and I will spare you the endless criticizing and speeches that came over the next several years. These things only pushed me farther away from her and further into my private desert wanderings. There was some part of me that wanted nothing to do with the kind of life either of my parents lived, but I had no clue as to how I could change anything.

I had been drinking beer and cheap wine since I was thirteen years old. I could probably blame that on my dad's influence, or even my mom, whose second husband owned a bar, but I knew I was responsible for my own choices. Not often but on occasion, a group of us would pool our monies and "acquire" the alcohol. The legal age to buy alcohol was 18, but a smart kid could easily get anything they wanted. By the time I was sixteen I added smoking pot, and by seventeen taking pills…and more. I was already spending time in local bars to hear all kinds of rock, blues or bluegrass bands and went to my first large arena concert in December, 1976. I saw Black Sabbath at Madison Square Garden, next came Pink Floyd, Grateful Dead then Neil Young and I was hooked.

I listened to pretty much any genre and started building a nice collection of albums. Even the music I chose to listen to held threads of God's tapestry. I could identify with many of the singer-songwriters and musicians who seemed to be traveling the same road as me, questioning beliefs and searching for love and the truth of our existence and hoping there was a merciful God up there. Working in a record store, I always had access to the genre of Christian music, but there was slim pickin's as far as variety or style back then and not much room for sinners. Thank God that genre has gone through a metamorphosis over the years. But at that time in my life, I found a place of comfort in rock bands like Hot Tuna, who sometimes played old blues tunes written by Reverend Gary Davis, or sometimes rocked out with Papa John Creach on a most wickedly played violin. There was nothing better for deep thought or pure escapism, than friends and music…and a few drinks or a toke were an added bonus.

For much more than a decade, my life consisted of working all day listening to music and then heading out with friends, listen to more music and maybe get high if we could. If I had vacation or a long weekend, I would go camping with friends in Upstate NY, or even the Adirondacks. Whenever I was out in nature, I felt happy and free and saw glimpses of God in all things. I didn't have teen angst, instead I saw the good side of things and possibilities, but I didn't have the confidence to turn from things that held me back. I had not learned yet how to step out in faith. God was there with me but I didn't know it and I didn't know *He was willing to help me*. So I clung to whatever felt good or resembled love. For me it was lots of friends, concerts or bars, camping trips, drugs and looking for love in all the wrong places. I did a few things that could have gotten me arrested and by the grace of God, I managed to avoid being in a physical prison.

My mom would say, (As if lost in a desert!) I was wandering through life aimlessly. I could argue that I *was* aimed, but just not at the target she wanted me to hit.

I probably had more guy friends than girl friends, and I must say that I knew some truly good hearted people. As far as the guys in my life and I admit there were quite a few, I had true feelings for them, but I was never able to commit to a relationship longer than a few months. Then of course the ones that I fell for the hardest could not commit to me. Maybe they thought I was too wacky or possibly unstable? Who knows…?

I met my best and lifelong friend when I had a party and invited a guy with whom I was hoping to become more than friends but he brought a date! This was his new girlfriend and I wanted to hate her but she was incredibly nice and we wound up as best friends. Years after that party she wound up introducing me to the guy who would become my husband. Still later, my husband and I were divorced, but I am still friends with that girl to this day. I truly loved my husband but as it turned out, we were both broken by things which happened to us in our lives that were not under our control. He was the first person who I could actually imagine myself with as we would grow old and grey. He was a guitar player in a band when I met him, I didn't even know if he had a "real" job and I didn't care. Later I found out he worked on Wall Street, but you wouldn't know it by the looks of him. He was funny, good looking, liked music, motorcycles, and had hair longer than mine which he kept in a ponytail. If you work in the research department on Wall Street no one cares if you wear a suit and tie. The one thing about him that I was warned about but ignored was his temper and that he was very controlling. I will just say that I thought my love for him was going to conquer that temper and things would be great, but without knowing and understanding where his anger came from, I seemed to escalate it instead.

The worse things got, the more I would drink and that was not good for either of us. By the end of our first year together it got to a point where I was in tears almost daily and I could not see how anything would change unless I left him. So one morning after he left for work, I had a good friend who helped me move out and she gave me a place to stay until I could figure some things out. I would not let myself live in fear like my mom did, so a few months later we were divorced. We saw each other from time to time afterwards and were able to remain friends but went on separately with our lives.

Years later, as I was packing some of my mom's things because she was moving again, I came across a remembrance book from my parents honeymoon. It was a wooden book tied together with leather strings and had their names burned into the wood. My mom and dad spent their honeymoon at Echo Valley Lodge in the Pocono Mountains in 1954.

On the first page of the book there were signatures of other couples who they spent time with at the lodge, and I saw my husband's first and last name. That was weird. Then there was a photo of mom, dad, and the other couples in front of small airplane. I was looking at a familiar face but it was neither of my parents. I was looking at my husband's father and mother on their honeymoon and she was wearing the ring that I wore on my wedding day. There were several photos of both our parents enjoying their time together. It's funny that neither my husband nor I knew this before we met. I guess our parents didn't keep in touch after that time, otherwise someone would have recalled the names and faces when we met and married nearly thirty years later. It did seem so strange though as if it was God's plan for us to meet. My husband's mother had a debilitating disease and he helped care for her through most of his youth. She had already passed away before I met him.

No matter how much we love someone, it can weigh heavily on the caregivers if we don't understand how to rely the Lord's strength in our weakness, especially if the caregivers are the children. That's something I wish I understood when my sisters and I needed to care for our own parents as they suffered terminal illness. My husband's father eventually remarried and I was first introduced to him when we went to visit him in the hospital after he suffered a heart attack.

You never know what another person has had to deal with in their lifetime which can have some serious impact on the temperament of that person. People can not change each other, but with God, all things are possible.

Jesus looked at them and said, "With man this is impossible, but with God all things are possible." Matthew 19:26 (AMPC)

That knowledge makes me hopeful that my ex-husband is out there somewhere enjoying a blessed life in Christ.

Aside from the divorce, my life continued down the same road without too much change from year to year. I wound up moving to an upstairs apartment in my mom's house. Maybe that was a mistake because we had what I would call a strained relationship. From my perspective there was just no pleasing her. It was more like appeasement and later when she was ill, it became hard to know if her complaints of pain were sincere or more manipulative cries for attention. She had been through a few operations and a list of medical conditions over those years, which came one after the other. She had a blocked carotid artery, uterine cancer, diabetes, with glaucoma and thyroid issues, limb swelling and a nervous skin condition to name a few.

My sisters, who were living elsewhere, helped taking turns going back and forth to the hospitals and appointments until she was well enough each time to be at home. After a while she decided to sell her house and move to a retirement village near my younger sister. I remained in the same neighborhood but found a new apartment.

After I was moved in and settled for a while, I was cleaning a small window which looked out on the alleyway of the house next door. On the windowsill was an old crucifix which was made in Germany. It was tied on a lavender ribbon, like a gift. I asked the landlord if he knew where it came from, but he had no idea and didn't think it belonged to the prior tenants. It was larger than average, like the kind a nun would wear. It was very old by appearance, made with wood and metal and I liked it very much so I put it in a small pouch for safe keeping. I felt as if it was left there on purpose for me as a sign that someone was watching over me. It was one of those odd things and seemed coincidental, that just when I was feeling alone, I found reassurance in the cross.

Around that same time the company I worked for merged with another one, and since I was making the same salary that their managers made, they decided I would have to go into management and take on more responsibility for the same money. I could see the responsibility and stress the managers had to deal with and I avoided it for as long as possible. I said no to that deal and they fired me on a technicality, which I fought and got a small severance pay deal.

Eventually I did go into management for another company at a music store on 33rd St. in NYC. It was more money and the city can be fun, but I hated the traveling, especially on the subway late at night. Time passed and I was promoted to a larger store across from Bloomingdale's. It was the same old job with new friends and new stress. Music stores are generally a cool, crazy, fun place to work. In NYC, you get to meet a mixed bag of people from all over the world and plenty of celebrities stop in to browse. Stores are conveniently located by subway entrances which provide easy access for the customers. This access unfortunately provides a convenient getaway for criminals. Everyday was a new adventure in loss prevention.

This particular store had three levels, so we had several managers to cover the different music categories. Because of the location, there were several robberies even before I came to work there. Then one day I was doing an all day shift because of a routine audit, and two other managers were set to close the store. I stayed longer than usual because of the audit, but decided not to stay for closing. Just a short while after I left the building, they closed the store but were unaware that there were three gunmen hiding in a utility closet. The gunmen tied everyone up, taped their mouths shut and put them face down on the floor. I can only imagine what went through their minds as they waited. They forced the manager to open the safe and give them the cash. I certainly did thank God, that when the gunmen left no one was injured. The robbers were never caught as far as I know.

Probably another year went by and things seemed fine. One morning I was on my way to the store room to place an order for merchandise and I stopped, smiled and asked if a customer if he needed any help. He said no thanks, he found what he needed and he smiled back, so I continued to the store room.

Maybe five minutes later as I reached for the phone to call in the order, I saw the assistant manager with an odd look on his face and then I saw the taller man in back of him with a gun in held to his back. It was the customer who I just spoke with on the sales floor. I just stared frozen in disbelief. The man pointed the gun at me and told me to get the money. So I got up and went to the safe to open it, but I had trouble with the combination the first time because I was nervous. He said loudly but calmly to get it open now. I was able to open it on the second try and put whatever money I could grab, into his backpack, including the rolled coins.

Then he told us to get against the wall and take off our clothes. I have to say I was not sure at all if this was the end or just the start of whatever he had planned.

I was visibly upset and shakily trying to speak, but then he said *"not-gonna-rape-ya-nuthin' jus-take-of-ya-clothes"*. I got as far as my underwear and the same for the other manager, and then as the gunman started to leave he said "don'-come-ou-thadoor-or-ahma-busta-cap-in-yo-ass". Translated from Ebonics that's "stay or I'll shoot". As he walked out of the store room an employee was on her way in and the gunman said, "Oh, I was just talking with the managers" and he laughed and kept going. She looked confused as she saw us half dressed, but with the safe opened, she knew what just happened.

I called the upper level and told the employee at the door to not look directly at the man I described coming up the stairs, but to let me know when he was outside the building and what direction he went. We called the police and they also called an ambulance because I had some chest pains. They found I had some prior damage to my heart but I felt fine, so I opted not to go to the hospital. A bit later the police brought us to the precinct to look through books of mug shots to try to I.D. the gunman. We had no luck with that and I don't think he was ever caught.

There had been other robberies that same year in the city where things turned out a lot worse. I know the

Lord had me under His wings for both those robberies at our store. I would have been there for the first robbery but something made me decide not to stay. The second robbery could have gone horribly wrong because just two days prior, we had the safe repaired...the lock kept getting stuck and was *nearly impossible* to open even without being shaky. In addition, I decided that morning to take the last night's deposit to the bank early instead of waiting for the next shift manager who was running late, so all the robber got was the basic funds on hand. Sure you can say it was just coincidence, but then I would still thank God for the coincidences, because I have had *thousands* of coincidences happen in my life to date.

Soon after that my dad passed away. He had been in and out of the V.A. hospital many times over the years for heart attacks, all related to his alcoholism. He never went there willingly, always waited till he collapsed. My older sister would usually wind up driving all over Manhattan to try and get him help. Hard as he tried to stay sober, he never made it more than a year at a time before he was drinking just as heavily or worse than before.

He basically had to retire early and was collecting his pension but that did not quite meet the demands of his addiction. He was still caring for his sister, and by then he had two more ex-wives, but I did not keep up much with his activities. He once drank a bottle of antiseptic mouthwash for the alcohol content and that put him back in the hospital. It is a hard thing to watch someone die slowly from alcohol.

I used to imagine with all his talents, what he could have achieved and what a better life he could have had, but he just became a depressed, old, drunken, broken man. We did what we could to help him, but his problems were a deeper burden than any of us knew how to bear and he refused professional help for any longer than it took to become sober again.

Around Thanksgiving 1996, his sister passed away and he really spiraled downward. Even before this he would walk around with blood coming out of his body in chunks and still he did not or could not stop drinking. Sometimes I had to leave work and go help him, but it was becoming too much for me to deal with and our busy holiday season had already started. My boss did not seem to understand what I was going through until I brought a pair of my dad's blood-caked pants in to show her. The fact that I did that should show you my state of mind was a little dark and cloudy with a chance of rain.

He turned sixty-five years old that December and before he could even cash his first Social Security check, the call came on Christmas Eve while I was at work. My dad collapsed and had a heart attack on the street outside of a bar and was brought to the hospital. About an hour or so later there was another call to say he had passed away. At first I used to think that this was his last mean thing to do to his family...dying on Christmas Eve...yeah, thanks for that memory Dad. But I began to feel so sorry for him when I thought about what it might be like to be him. When we were younger he would take us to church on Easter Sunday and then we would walk around the Ridgewood Reservoir, which maybe seems symbolic, being that the *water reserved for us,* was surrounded by a fence. Christ is the Living Water, but if the church fences you out saying you are no longer welcomed there, how do you get to drink the cup of salvation and be forgiven?

Therefore with joy shall you draw water out of the wells of salvation.   Isaiah 12:3

The sorrows of death compassed me, and the pains of hell got hold on me: I found trouble and sorrow.

Then called I on the name of the LORD; O LORD, I beseech you, deliver my soul.

I will take the cup of salvation, and call on the name of the LORD.   Psalm 116:3,4,13 (AMPC)

He used to say a prayer every time he got in the car that the Lord might keep him safe from hurting anyone. One time he told me he shot a mouse and he cried long and hard about that incident. He showed remorse...over a mouse! I believe he was being remorseful for much more than that mouse. He believed in God, but he felt condemned and unworthy like me and so many others have been falsely led to believe, we were unforgivable. He never understood the unconditional love, forgiveness and help available to all of us through our relationship with Jesus Christ. When we know who we are in Christ, we can overcome anything because He is our unlimited resource. Now I believe my dad died on Christmas Eve because the Lord had mercy and took him home to rest until we are all together again as one in Christ.

Come to Me, all you who labor and are heavy-laden and overburdened, and I will cause you to rest. [I will ease and relieve and refresh your souls.]

***Take My yoke upon you and learn of Me, for I am gentle (meek) and humble (lowly) in heart, and you will find rest (relief and ease and refreshment and recreation and blessed quiet) for your soul* Matthew 11:28-29 (AMPC)**

An autopsy was needed before they could release my dad's body for burial but that was not happening anytime soon because of the holidays. So I took time off from work to get through that and to see my family. When you take yourself out of a situation, you have time to get a little clarity of mind. I really needed that break to see that I wanted and needed to make some changes in my life. I knew for sure I wanted *not* to drink and to find a new job somewhere *not* in the city.

4- EXODUS FOR A PARTY OF ONE

And they wandered about from nation to nation,
From one kingdom to another people.   Proverbs 105:13

My older sister had been living in Westchester, NY, where she owned a condominium and her soon to be husband also had a condo not too far away. Since they were looking to buy a house together, she moved into his condo and put hers up for sale. Unfortunately for her, the market was really bad for sellers and she was going to have to take loss if it didn't go up soon.

While it was on the market, it just so happened that I was interviewing with another company who asked if I would be willing to relocate, with one of the options being in Port Chester, NY. My sister offered that I could stay in her condo which was not far from Port Chester, while I looked for a more permanent place. I took the job and moved after I trained for three months in their Manhattan location.

One of the reasons I was hired for this location, was to try and clean it up, as it was losing money due to high theft and poor management. Fixing stores was something I seemed to be good at, so not only was I able to get rid of the theft, but in less than a year I had the store making sixteen percent over the sales projection. I even earned a large bonus, which they would give out in the Spring after the holiday season. But... this job took up every bit of my time and energy. There were many confrontations involving police to get rid of the external theft problems, plus there were several years of backlogged shipping paperwork that had to be sorted out.

I really did nothing else but work and eat and get a little sleep. So of course, I wound up coming down with some kind of super-bug-flu-virus-dizzy-puking-thing and I could not even stand up without falling over. I was too sick to get myself to a doctor and I didn't really have anybody in my life that was able to come help me, so I was forced to stay in bed or crawl until I had the strength to get up again.

I found out later, my district manager was holding back payroll hours every week, which I was entitled to use to meet the new sales demand. I could have hired two or three people with those hours and maybe got a few hour of much needed rest. Instead it went to his pocket as a payroll bonus. I had heard rumors about this district manager's shady behavior but now I was living with it. A year of working under his thumb proved too stressful for me. Things grew worse because I went over his head to speak with the regional director about the situation and got my deserved hours, but now he seemed intent on making things unnecessarily difficult for me.

There's a point where you know something is going to break and I knew it was going to be me, so I handed my keys to my assistant and walked out, leaving that big bonus behind. I have always been a believer that money isn't everything. My family didn't always see it that way but I knew what had to be done if I was to keep my health or sanity.

It wasn't long before I was back to work. A children's educational toy company was opening a brand new store about half a mile from where I was living. By that time I had gained a lot of experience, so I was hired almost immediately to train in one store, while the new one was being built. I know the Lord's hand was in what happened next because I completed training ahead of schedule and they decided I should go to Long Island, NY, to one of the larger stores. It was almost an hour and a half commute in good weather, while I could actually walk from home to the other store that was being built. I agreed to do as they asked but mentioned that eventually I would like a store closer to home. Just before I was about to start at the Long Island store, I got a call from my boss who managed to make a few changes in personnel and I got the new store in Westchester!

I was there all through the building process, plus hiring, training and stocking, and it was a beautiful store. Unfortunately during the set up, I had some injury to my back from helping unloaded thousands of boxes off the trucks, but it wasn't going to keep me from enjoying my new store. I was sober and making good money and things were looking up. Even my family approved of this move and it was timely that I should be in a children's educational toy store because both my sisters now had young children. I was an aunt to two nephews and a niece! My mom even loaned me a down payment so I could afford to purchase my sister's condo at a great price. My older sister walked me through all the legal paperwork and she was actually patient, understanding, and a great help to me in getting the mortgage approved.

Focusing on work kept me pretty happy for the next few years and I made some wonderful friends through that time. I had an especially bright and cheery assistant manager and I came to rely on her a lot through our years working together. It was that feeling again, as if certain people were in my life for a reason. She had strong faith and it was evident in her demeanor and how she handled difficult situations with a positive attitude. In retail you wind up working all the holidays when others are with their families, so sometimes the people you work with become family. You know what's going on in their lives because you spend half your days together and you care about their happiness.

When I was younger I didn't mind working all the time, because I wasn't getting along with my family, but things can change as you get older and with my sisters having their own families now it seemed to change them a little. Maybe more time away from our parents influence had helped us all grow a little closer to each other. It was still a rocky road but we did love each other and had begun to figure out the bad habits or negative issues we faced had more to do with our parent's relationships than they did with our own.

After a few years working in this company which had already opened several new stores with plans to open more, a decision was made to merge with a competitor and become one large more powerful company. I don't pretend to know a great deal about corporate mergers but I do know having gone through it before, when a *family owned* company such as the one I had been working for, merges with another one or brings in outsiders to help run things, they don't necessarily act as reinforcements. They can weaken the integrity of the structure and things can deteriorate and collapse. My thinking was as the saying goes, *if it ain't broke, don't fix it*!

But they did merge and as a result, my smaller new store was closed because it was right down the road from the larger store which belonged to the other merge partner. So they transferred me down the road and once again, I became the manger of a store that already had a great deal of internal and external theft of money and merchandise. They fired the old manager because of it and sent me into the wilderness of this store that had a completely different operating system, armed only with a manual to figure it all out. Fortunately I'm a pretty patient person, which is what you need to be if you deal with the public in a customer service position. However, since the previous manager let chaos rule, I was perceived as a threat to the current employees who all thought I would fire them.

As I patiently retrained the good, weeded out the bad, some of them got very ugly, and I had to battle against attempts of sabotage almost daily. Someone went as far as to put boards spiked with nails under my car tires in hopes of either having them blow out or cause me to crash. Once again I knew the Lord was with me, because I got in my car and then decided to go back and check on something and that's when I spotted the nails glimmering under the car. For over a month afterward the company hired police to be present in the store while I continued to make changes to the personnel.

When things were finally running well enough to maybe take two days off in a row, there came the acquisitions. Now the two toy stores who merged to become a super-store, wanted to acquire not one but two more companies who had related merchandise, and have a mega-mega- store with four themes. This expansion was all done in a very short period of time and everyone except the people in charge could see this was overkill. Or they knew and didn't care. A few people at the top make large amounts of money and then they go away leaving the rest of the crew trying to keep the ship afloat. In the five years I was with that company, there were as many changes in policies and procedures as there were to the merchandise and designs of the interiors and exteriors of the stores.

That is a lot to handle alongside of the day to day running of the store. It's not good for the customers either. We had an established brand and a good rapport with our customers and now there were constant changes in merchandise, layouts, even contradictions in how we were to serve or not serve the customer. Stressful!

I was having more pain in my back more frequently and it was slowing me down quite a bit. I was using a cane and my boss told me to hide it whenever upper management came in for a visit. I was seeing a specialist for heat therapy treatments with an option for surgery but I had seen what happened to other mangers who took recovery time off from work. They were told their jobs would still be there but somehow it fell through one of those *loopholes*. So I just pushed through each day as best as I could. I knew my condition was getting serious and I was taking pain killers on a regular basis and some of them caused blistering on my legs so it was difficult to find the correct medication. I had put on quite a bit of weight. I had a lot of swelling with the pain in my legs and sometimes in even my arms. I thought the swelling was from the medication or maybe the wine I had started to drink again just to relax after work. Yes…that was not a wise decision…thanks for pointing that out!

I was also finding it harder to breathe and was using my asthma inhaler much more than recommended. For sure I wasn't eating right or getting enough sleep, or restful sleep. There was always a new crisis at work and once again, it seemed all I did was work long hours and grab something to eat on the run, and then drink to relax. Oh…and I had another new habit… I didn't have a lot of time to shop so I ordered things from magazines which saved time and energy. I was making sufficient money so I figured I could afford to buy some things to show for all that job stress and aggravation. I was not even using most of the things I had already bought, but I just kept buying more. It was as if my brain didn't process that I didn't need these things, only that I needed something, and I settled for shopping. I bought more clothes just so I didn't have to trudge down to the condo laundry room drag it all back upstairs. Going up and down stairs had been hurting my joints more and more. I bought crock pots so I didn't have to stand there while things cooked.

So I was dealing with all that and then there was my mom who had been recently diagnosed with pancreatic cancer. I remember sitting on my couch half awake or drifting off and I saw a vision of my grandfather, Pop-Pop, standing there in his soldier uniform, and he said "***take care of her***", and I knew he meant my mom. Soon after she underwent a surgery called a Whipple Procedure to try to remove the cancerous tissue, but they found it wrapped all through her organs and could not proceed any further. They gave her four to six months to live if she refused to do chemotherapy but not much longer if she did it, so her choice was no chemo.

Through this next period in which she actually lasted nearly two more years, my mom was understandably scared and did some soul searching and turned to the Lord for comfort and it did help and change her. She listened to sermons from Dr. Charles Stanley on television or radio. We had some personal conversations and she told me she was sorry about the way she had treated me over the years and she said she knew I had a good heart. That meant more to me than anything she ever gave me.

Then she did something that surprised me very much. I had been running up a lot of bills and not really keeping track or even taking time to balance my checkbook properly. When I started to realize how much debt I was accumulating. I got a little nervous, OK a lot nervous, as to how I was going to pay bills or my mortgage if something should happen and I lost my job. It was already becoming a problem to make my monthly budget work. Yes, I was helping create my own stress! So I found a credit management program which consolidated my bills and I started paying down the debt but it was going to take several years and of course I had to stop spending. I managed to pay about twenty percent of the total, but it was very difficult.

Even though I was making payments, the creditors liked to call every day to remind me how much I owed. I hated to hear the phone ring. I hated the job stress and in general I hated the way I was feeling drained and in pain all the time while trying to appear happy for the customers and my staff.

During an overnight visit with my mom, as we were talking and as sick as she was, she could see I was not doing well physically and probably mentally. I think she already knew, but I told her what was going on and I could see she had actual concern for me. No lectures, just concern. She told me she had a will made out and for a long time I was not in it, because she thought I would be like my father and spend it all on alcohol. In my head I thought of the irony, since her behavior toward me was the main reason I started to drink. But as I said, she was changing since renewing her faith and she saw a different side of me, and this was showing me a different side of her. She offered to pay the balance of my debt, which was several thousand dollars. She thought instead of waiting till she died, that it would be more useful to share with me while she was still around. We had a Kleenex moment. (Kleenex tissues, tears, hugs, get it?)

Believe me when I say that only the Lord can change people. He worked through my mom and took that burden from me.

A new heart also will I give you, and a new spirit will I put within you: and I will take away the stony heart out of your flesh, and I will give you an heart of flesh. Ezekiel 36:26 (APMC)

There was forgiveness between both of us because I surely was a rebellious child during her days of rule over me. I tried to drive up and spend time with her and stay overnight if I could be off from work, but I was really feeling ineffective at doing anything more. On one trip, to meet with my sisters and a nurse so we could talk about what to expect from the progression of my mom's cancer, I could not keep awake while the nurse was speaking. I mean this literally. I tried to keep my attention on her and keep my eyes opened, but over and over I felt myself start to fall over, only to jolt awake and find everyone staring at me. The nurse asked if I had narcolepsy and I told her no, but I was just so exhausted and was not sleeping enough.

I didn't know I had some other medical issues that were not yet diagnosed. I was rarely able to sleep more than two hours consecutively and I was having pinched nerve pain in my arms and legs pretty often, which I attributed to stress. My legs were always swollen even with taking blood pressure medication to reduce the water in my body. I figured this was from standing on the sales floor all day at work. Though it was difficult I was able to get the job done and pretend to be happy, but there were fewer and fewer days of feeling healthy.

The one advantage of not sleeping was I could sit up all night and watch over my mom. She had a fear of not waking up if she slept, and it comforted her to have someone sitting nearby and rub her back and legs which were in pain. One sister would visit in the daytime and I took the nighttime shift. Eventually her condition worsened and my sister found a wonderful hospice that had a caring staff. Her room had a large window overlooking the water, so mom would have something peaceful to look at while she was there.

When I was at home it was my habit to keep the news on the television for company. So the morning of September 11th 2001, started as just another day and it was one of those beautiful clear autumn days. I was watching Mike Sheehan, on Fox News, who was reporting and pointing to something that hit the top of the World Trade Center, and we could see smoke coming off the tower. I thought it might be another helicopter crash, because that's happened before. He kept reporting while others were on the way to the scene when something hit the second tower. Some kind of shock wave flashed through my body and I thought we must be at war. I was just glued there staring at the TV with my face contorted in disbelief as I listened and watched the horror happening. When we began to realize what was going on and evacuations were underway, I called my best friend who travels by subway through there every day, to see if she was OK. There was no answer and all I could do was leave a message. I called my store and told them to put on the radio on and then call the night crew and tell them not to come in.

After the towers collapsed, normal things no longer made sense and we got the OK to close down the store and find a way to send everyone home safely. Later that night I finally heard from my friend who was on the *last train* that made it trough the station before the collapse. She was with all the others evacuating the city that day, through the devastation, covered in dusty muck with wet streams of tears and faces of confusion, walking silently over the bridge and eventually home.

It wasn't until some time later that we found out our friend of many years, fire fighter Lt. Steve Bates, from Engine 235 out of Brooklyn, was one of those heroes who gave his life to help others during that heinous attack. For weeks we kept a radio on in the office at the store, because things don't just go back to normal after an attack of that magnitude. There was a lot of restlessness in the air as people tried to cope with everything ongoing and related to September, 11th 2001.

I tried to explain what was happening to my mom but none of it really mattered to her because she was near the end of her life and not able to focus more than a few minutes at a time.

She passed away just weeks later on October 28th 2001. It was her wish to be cremated, so that is what we did and my younger sister keeps our mom's urn of ashes at her home. It took quite a while before I stopped thinking, "I gotta call Mom and tell her…Oh…"…and then I'm sad for a second, then I look upward and tell her anyway. My sisters and I still talk to Mom's urn from time to time or joke that she looks a little dusty.

Soon after her passing I was right back to work and not in any better shape. I was physically and mentally exhausted and now there were rumors the company was filing for *Chapter 11*, which means bankrupt and probably going out of business. It's not like we didn't see it coming. The company was spending money on frivolous things like unnecessary renovations and signs and special meetings with fancy catering. These are things that run up the tabs, money they know they won't have to pay back, because when they file for Chapter 11, they are protected from the creditors. Of course the company denies everything right up until they ask you to sign an agreement to stay through the store closings, so they can avoid everyone running out at the same time. I agreed to stay on as long as it took, which was over a year. In that time something happened that was going to become a huge problem for me down the road.

I had a small patch on my lower left leg which was a leftover scar from a severe case of poison ivy. I got a mosquito bite or a bee sting in that exact spot and I quickly bent over and scratched at it with my fingernails. A little later I realized I had scratched it open enough to make it bleed, so I washed it and put a bandage over it, and forgot about it. Still later I noticed my sock was wet when I took it off and I could see that it was actually soaked with liquid. It wasn't blood, just clear liquid. I assumed this was just extra water in my body even though I took prescribed water pills which helped keep my blood pressure down. I washed the wound, used antiseptic and bandaged it again so I could go to work. I didn't feel anything leaking but by the time I got to work, my sock and pants leg were already soaked through that area. I was a little stressed over it but I rolled up some paper towels and stuffed it under the bandage until I could get home after work.

I thought maybe this was leaking because of the pressure from standing on my feet all day. So I used some triple antibacterial ointment which helps to heal faster, wrapped the leg and stayed off my feet for the rest of the day and over night. I did this each night over the next week as a precaution and I thought it was healed because the leaking had stopped. I really didn't want to see another doctor, because it was enough that I had back pain, sciatica, asthma, high blood pressure and significant weight gain. I didn't even recognize me anymore. Everything seemed to be getting worse at the same time and at the worse possible time. I started thinking that maybe the store closing was a blessing in disguise. I'd be out of a job, but I'd have a chance to concentrate on my health and take my time to find a new job. I knew I did not want to be working in retail on the sales floor on my feet forever. I thought about taking a year off after the store closed and maybe take a few continuing education classes at Westchester Community College.

I went to visit my sisters and told them about the store closing and some of the details, but I didn't mention the classes or taking a year off because they were only concerned that I get right back out there and get a job. It became my habit not to tell people too many details of what was going on in my life because they always had a quick answer and expected that I do exactly what they thought was right for me. During the visit, I noticed my sister's dog kept coming over to me trying to lick my leg at that spot which I thought was healed. I was hoping nobody would notice and I think nobody did.

As the weeks and months went on, we started having special closing sales. I was barely able to get through a day without taking many prescribed and over the counter pain medications. One day the phone rang and as I went to answer it, I tripped and fell slamming my leg on a table and then just sat on the floor thinking of that stupid commercial...I was the old lady who fell and couldn't get up!

I called my assistant into work quite a few days to cover for me when I just couldn't get myself out of bed because everything hurt so badly. My legs were swollen, dark reddish, hot and my whole body was swelling up and I just looked huge. I wasn't getting any exercise, other than working all day but that is pain and stress, not exercise. At home I was just too tired to cook. I ate drive-through food with a bottle of wine hoping it would help me feel relaxed. I pretended to be fine if someone asked, but I was not fine at all and it was too embarrassing to even try to make sense of how I got this way. I was extremely overweight but I could not convince myself it was just improper diet like my family seemed to think.

Finally the store was closed and I made it through all the chaos. It was one of the most stressful periods of my life. I found out my boss had a heart attack just weeks later. I don't know all of his medical issues but I know he was also under a lot of pressure and had an autistic child at home who would need costly special care in life. Thankfully he survived the attack.

Within a week or two after the store closed I had time to get my resume together and scout out a few job possibilities. I had plenty of experience and a good record with great references, but I could see as I sat through the interviews that I was not going to get a position anytime soon. I had interviewed and or hired hundreds of employees over the years, so I knew what employers were looking for in a potential manager. On paper I looked great, but in person even though I had good questions and answers, I was a physical mess. I was huge and walked painfully slow with a cane. Even I wouldn't hire me for retail management.

I did actually have one company call me to start work nearly six weeks after I interviewed. This company owner happened to be friends with the owner of the first toy store I managed. He gave me a great recommendation, but he had not seen me in years. Unfortunately it came after I had already made the decision to first take some continuing education classes and then sell the condo and move somewhere in Upstate NY. I knew in my heart I could not handle the position he offered and I think he had doubts as well, which is why even with the recommendation, he took that long to get back to me.

On the night I made my decision to sell the condo, I had a very vivid dream. I saw a beautiful healthy green vine that was growing and spread across the wall as one, two, three, four bright red roses each blossomed in sequence and then it faded away. I was in awe and I felt happy. I knew I was entering a new chapter of my life.

5- ACCIDENTALLY GETTING BORN AGAIN

I have gone astray like a lost sheep; seek Your servant, For I do not forget Your commandments

Proverbs 119:176 (AMPC)

Not having a job can be a major cause of stress if you don't have a lead on a new position or an alternative plan. Fortunately for me someone was guiding me even if I didn't know it yet. I felt strongly about taking classes to reinforce my skills and prepare for something new. I applied for unemployment and signed up for some basic brush up classes for computer, Spanish and QuickBooks. The classes were only a few days a week and I could finally get in some sort of sleep pattern, so I had a little more energy but not much.

I began to look online for a place to live in Upstate NY and I was pleased to find there were a few different properties which I could afford. My younger sister and her husband owned a condo on Hunter Mountain, so I looked at properties near there, but somehow the ones I liked and could afford were about an hour north of there.

I really didn't care about finding a job, because I knew first I needed to get away from where I was, both physically and mentally. I started slowly cleaning up my condo which had amassed a ton of junk and garbage which was piled up everywhere. It looked like one of those hoarder shows on television. There was so much of it that I wound up giving away seven large size trash bags of clothes and miscellaneous items just to make room to get organized again. All the while I'd been working, dealing with health issues, my mom, my grief and everything else, I'd let everything at home get out of hand.

It took many months of sorting out, throwing out and packing up to get the place ready to list on the market. I hired someone to paint and do small repairs because I was in no shape to do that work myself. By that time I was running out of money and had to borrow from a friend and my family to keep my mortgage payments up to date and I was living on vitamins and bologna sandwiches.

I looked for part-time work while my condo was on the

market to be sold and was able to find temporary desk work at a small publishing and distribution company in Armonk. I almost had to turn down the job because the office was three flights up and I couldn't walk up steps without severe pain. Fortunately the woman who hired me understood the situation and told me I could use the freight elevator. I thanked her with tears in my eyes because there are not many people in a hiring position who see beyond physical appearance.

There were daytime, evening and night shifts and I worked the day shift. Since I was only going to be there a few months I didn't do much talking about all the things going on in my life to the few friends I made there. During my last week as the shifts were changing, one of the women on the evening shift was sitting at a desk with a deck of tarot cards and doing a reading for a co-worker. Another woman explained to me that she did these readings for free. She and her mother both had a gift for tarot readings and didn't think it was right to charge money for this gift. Then the woman asked me if I wanted a reading. I said no at first but when asked once more, I said ok.

I never met this woman before and my co-workers knew almost nothing about me that they could have shared with her, other than I planned on moving when my condo sold. She started by asking if there was anything in particular I wanted to know. I told her I was planning on moving and wanted to know how that might work out. She flipped a few cards and told me the focus was around someone who was very sick. I told her (which I knew) that was me, and I did not want to know about sickness. She flipped a few more cards and went on to tell me in great detail about some interactions between me and my two sisters and some other personal details. She was amazingly accurate in what she told me and I know she could not have come by this information any other way except that she did indeed have a gift.

It was almost unbelievable, but I felt that this message was there at that time to help me have hope, even though I knew I was ill. She asked me if there was anything else specific that I wanted to know. Considering all that I had been through in my life, all I wanted to know was, "Will I be happy"? She flipped more cards and had a look of sheer surprise on her face when she said, "Not only will you be happy but you will have a relationship which brings you great joy". I told her that I didn't know anyone at all where I was planning to move, except for the real estate person and she was a woman. So I laughed and asked, "Am I going to become a lesbian"? She told me "No, in this relationship he is someone you work for". So again, I laughed and said "Well maybe I'll find a job and fall in love with the boss". Then she told me "This is someone you already know". I insisted, "Really, I don't know anyone where I'm going, but we'll see what happens I guess". The session ended and everything was 100% accurate, although that last part, I felt certain she had misread my cards or they were maybe for the person sitting next to me. I will come back to this reading a bit later in the book, because this tarot reading happened in December, 2004 and I officially moved in September of 2005. The things she described either happened or were happening except that last relationship part, so I tucked that prediction in a little compartment somewhere in the back of my mind.

During the next few months I kept looking for a new property online and found a few I could probably afford when the condo sold. I didn't have the money yet to put down as a deposit, so there wasn't much I could do but wait. I knew there would be an in-between time where I would be temporarily homeless, but my older sister and her husband could see that I was determined to move so they generously offered that I could live with them while finding a new place to live. I'm sure it was not convenient to have me there but they made a genuine effort to make a nice comfortable space for me. It took another three months to find a buyer for the condo and then sign all the paperwork at the closing, but it did finally happen, again with my sister's help.

Meanwhile my younger sister helped me with packing up whatever was not going into storage and she helped do most of the cleaning up afterward, because I was having a lot of breathing problems and back pain and it was difficult to even load my car for the drive. At that time, I had a better relationship with my younger sister, perhaps because older sisters in general or at least in our case seemed to believe they were in charge of the younger ones…even after they became adults. We could commiserate once in a while when the older sister gave us younger ones grief, we would laugh together saying "You're not the boss of me"! In any case, I could not have done all those things by myself and I was amazed that my sisters along with their husbands were helping me through this move.

It is not an easy task to write about the past strained relationship the three of us sisters had together. Especially since it is not at all how we are with each other now and that is something for which I give my many thanks to God.

As I see it, so much of our anger, frustration, and hurt was caused by the way were influenced by or treated by our parents, which developed and emerged as stubborn, prideful, and spiteful behavior at times. We didn't grow in an atmosphere of mutual support, building up, or sharing joy in one another's achievements.

I can't say how each of them *actually* felt about me, but I felt unaccepted most of the time because I didn't prioritize things the same way, share the same views on what it meant to be successful in life and it seemed my opinion had no value. I know that I did love them but in my heart I believed I was more of a family obligation to them instead of an equally loved sibling or child. I shared less and less of the personal details of my life over the years because again, I didn't think they valued anything I had to say, even in choosing my own career.

The reason for my writing about what is long since forgiven and changed, is to show that the seed of faith which God placed inside of us when we were first born and baptized, could not be stopped. Even when we give up, God does not give up on us. My relationship with God through Jesus Christ is my first priority now, because He has given me a whole new life and blessed me with a precious relationship with my two sisters and their families.

And he that sat on the throne said, Behold, I make all things new. And he said to me, Write: for these words are true and faithful.

Revelation 21:5 (AMPC)

It took nearly six months after I moved into my sister's house, before I was able to locate and finalize the purchase of a small house in Upstate NY. I knew I was not in good enough shape to find a job right away because my health was really declining, so I wanted to spend as little as possible while still having a decent place to live.

One of the first houses I looked at online that I could actually afford was already off the market with a buyer in contract when I asked to see it. I found a few other properties and drove up to have a look at them and see what else might be beneficial in the area. It was quite a long drive, nearly four hours and I had to stop a few times to stretch my legs because they were swollen and achy. I knew I could only make one or two trips in this condition, but the houses I saw were not what I had hoped for and I went back depressed and in pain. I think my sister wondered if I was going to be a permanent resident in her home. I didn't even tell her how hard the drive was and I just kept looking for other options.

Then something odd happened. When I checked the new listings, I saw the house I first liked was listed for sale again. I called the agent to confirm and she told me it was available. I wondered if there was something wrong with the property but she said no, the sale fell through because it needed to be an all cash sale, a mortgage was not approved. I went to see it and I felt like I was in the middle of nowhere which was a good thing. It was an older house but it seemed to be nicely rehabbed, on just over an acre with a tiny spring-water stream running through it. It was on the top of a mountain in a quiet little town with local markets and farms. It's funny that this town was only about seven blocks long through the village center and seemed like there was a church on every other block. I didn't have to think it over long at all. I felt it was where I needed to be, so I bought it and moved in on September 10th 2005.

The house was rehabbed but not completely finished. There were no appliances, or shelves in the closets or even a phone line which I found out after moving in that first day. When I first viewed the house it was filled with all kinds of antiques which belonged to the previous owner but I just assumed there would be a phone line! So with my cell phone that was now racking up what they called roaming charges, I called an electrician and phone company and had a working phone in a few days. Also, I switched phone carriers. After paying off the mortgage and my leftover debt, I had just enough to buy a decent used car and appliances for the new home, with some left for emergencies and taxes for a couple of years. Appliances came in the first week and I had fuel delivered for the stove and furnace.

I really loved to just go out and lean on the deck railing and look out at the hills and farms and the view of the sky was clear for nearly 360 degrees around. Every day I said, "Thank you God for getting me up here and letting me live here in peace for as long as that will be".

I felt sure I had cancer of some type but I did not want to get that confirmed. I certainly didn't want my family to know, so I thought I could just live here and slowly wither away and die surrounded by the beauty that God gave us. I kept a lot of pain medication around in case that time would come, at least it wouldn't be too painful, because I already I had enough pain in my life. When I drove down the road, sometimes I had to pull over and just cry. I knew I was sick but I was also happy to be here to see beauty of these mountains which made me feel somehow closer to God. Oh yeah, I forgot to mention this new place was smaller than my old place. So, my furniture was in storage until I could have a garage built to keep the hundreds of boxes which would otherwise be sitting on the lawn. Fortunately there was a nice Amish barn company who built and delivered a garage by November. Meanwhile I had an air mattress to sleep on and two upside down paint buckets for a computer table and chair. It was not an ideal situation. It took all my strength to unpack what little I brought up in the car. It hurt to stand too long, it hurt to sit too long and I felt like I was suffocating when I slept on the airbed. Getting up off the bed was killing my knees and so was going up and down the stairs.

My real-estate agent was a really nice woman with a family and she lived just a few miles from me. Being new to the neighborhood, she checked up on me and said to call if there was ever anything she could do and also let me know where to shop and find other things I might need. She even later introduced me to one of the local teens who did odd jobs like lawn mowing, building things that need to be put together, or even unloading the car for me when I shopped. So I felt good about living in this kind of town, but I started questioning how long I might be here. It was getting harder and harder to walk and it left me short of breath just to go down the driveway to the mailbox. Even driving the car was difficult now.

One morning as I was trying to get up off the airbed, I slipped and flopped back onto the bed and it burst open. I crash landed on the floor and the pain was shooting up my legs. I just sat there and wondered how I was going to get up. I had a tote nearby with cans of food and small kitchen appliances in it, so I managed to get near it and move it with my cane to a window and slowly painfully got to my feet. I was already taking ibuprofen and aspirin every few hours and now that wasn't even dulling the pain. You ever have one of those moments where you just think...what else can happen? Now what do I do?

I wondered how I could get something delivered immediately. Then I remembered that same website where I found someone to paint my old place, I could find some kind of used furniture quickly. Sure enough I found a couch big enough to sleep on. I already had a bed in storage but not a couch, so this would work. Was it a coincidence the owners lived just a few miles away so they were able to bring it to me in a couple of hours? I had only a bucket to sit on and there is no way I could sleep on the floor, so I was thankful for finding a couch. It was not at all my taste but it didn't matter at that point. I just needed to rest on something, and with a few sheets, pillows and a blanket I didn't notice how ugly it really was. Pretty soon the new garage would be built and in place, my boxes would be out of storage and I would have a real bed. But things started to go from bad worse *very* quickly.

That accident with the airbed must have done more damage than I knew or could see. My whole body was in pain and every movement was agonizing. I could not sleep at all; I was taking way too many pills and was feverish. It took me about an hour to get up, maneuver slowly down the hall to the bathroom and then back to the couch. Every time I had to get up I was in tears and I was drenched in sweat. I wasn't hungry and didn't want to move anymore. I only drank enough water to get the pills down without burning a hole in my throat or stomach lining. I cringed at the thought of having to get up again. Every muscle and nerve in my body felt like it was on fire. It was that way and getting worse for a nearly a week. I would fall in and out of consciousness long enough to take the pills, but walking to the bathroom had become an impossible task. I would sit on the toilet for at least an hour or longer crying and sweating profusely trying to gain enough strength to get to my feet by holding on to the washing machine so I didn't fall to the floor.

So I took all the medicine I had left in the bathroom and dragged it with some water back to the couch. Another day filled with that agony had passed and I was done. I could not take any more pain. There was no one for me to call and nothing I could to say to anyone. In that fevered state of mind I had no reason to believe that anyone would truly care. Family and friends all had their own problems they were dealing with and it didn't seem right to dump this on them. If the situation were reversed I know I would be the one saying, "Why didn't you just call me?" At that time, I loved my family but I never felt as though I was anything more than a family obligation to them. I *didn't* really want to die, but could not see past the physical pain anymore and I didn't want to pass my burden to them. I knew there was enough money in my account to cremate my remains if I was found. I must admit when I first thought of moving Upstate, I thought I could survive a few years but there was barely enough strength left in me to lie down on the couch and take the pills. I had fever and chills and was shaking in pain so bad that I knew I would not get up again and this would be my last night on earth. I had thousands of pills and took as many as I could at once without puking them up. I figured after a while I would take the rest of them because I would be well on my way by then and unable to vomit. So with tears in my eyes, I made the sign of the cross and prayed my last prayer.

"Dear Father in Heaven, I am so very sorry for this, I never thought my life would turn out this way. I wanted to do so many good things and now I can't even take care of myself anymore, please forgive me...Amen." I took a lot more pills, and then even more...---... ...-- -... ...---............

Cold…no…cool…what is that coolness on my hand?

My eyes opened and I turned my head to see the metal part of my cane had fallen onto my right hand and feeling the coolness of the metal woke me. I wondered how it moved from where it was and fell on me like it did. I had no idea of how much time had passed but I lifted my head and it didn't hurt so much anymore. I could move my legs and then I sat up. I just sat there in the quietness and wondered why I was awake. My fever was gone and I didn't have much pain. Slowly I tested my balance and found I could actually get up to my feet and inch my way around. I knew I wasn't dead but how could this be happening that I can stand up? I thought somehow it was my mother reaching from the other side of the great beyond, telling me to get up and live. I didn't understand exactly what happened and why I was alive but I felt it must have something to do with God, because I should have been dead.

I felt enough strength in my body that I was able to walk around slowly. I found something to eat and noticed my fever had completely gone. For the next few days I just kept wondering why I was still here and what do I do now? I was thanking God, but at the same time feeling very bad, very guilty, that I had tried to kill myself. My mind was still not clear but I knew I would not ever try that again because something was different.

I just kept going from day to day trying to eat more and sleep more, hoping I would gain more strength because I was still not able to go up or down stairs which meant I could not drive anywhere either. Fortunately I had no place to be, and I had food in the house or could have something sent. Now it was well into October, my new garage arrived and I was finally able to have my furniture delivered from storage. Except for whatever was essential, everything went into the garage, but now I had a real bed to sleep on and other furniture and curtains which made me feel hopeful that I might be around to enjoy my new home. I knew that I would eventually have to get out and find a doctor in the area. I wasn't feeling that I had strength yet to do much more than exist for the time being, but that is surely better than *not existing and not being*.

I had no idea that when I said my last prayer, it triggered something, opening the door to the One who was knocking, so to speak. Up until that point I was living my life in my own strength and trying to be good and failing, trying to be in control and losing it, trying to be independent and do everything without help, but wound up helpless. I was under the false impression that God only helps those who help themselves, which by the way, is NOT in the Bible. If they could help themselves, they wouldn't need God. I was an unworthy sinner and could no longer help myself so, what right would I have to ask God for help? It never occurred to me that I *could* ask. He designed us to be dependent on

Him alone and then firmly set on His foundation; He would lead the way to true prosperity, health and everlasting life.

God did not send Jesus for humanistic people who believe they need no help from Him or even deny His existence. They believe the welfare of all mankind is built from science and reasoning but give no acknowledgement to the One who supplied the building materials. What would be the point to rescue someone who doesn't know or admit they are dying? He sent Jesus to save the imperfect believers, wandering sheep, lost sinners, the sick, the poor, the rejected, the helpless and hopeless, because He loves us all.

When I prayed for forgiveness and confessed that I couldn't take care of myself, I was actually surrendering my life and accidentally invited Him to save me. In that moment as I gave up my independence, I became totally dependent on Christ.

Even so, it took quite a long while before I could figure that out and start cooperating with His plan for my life. He had a plan for me even before I was born and when I was baptized, He was with me and began to teach me, but I wasn't aware I should be paying attention or that I was a student.

The sorrows of death compassed me, and the pains of hell got hold on me: I found trouble and sorrow.

Then called I on the name of the LORD; O LORD, I beseech you, deliver my soul.

I will take the cup of salvation, and call on the name of the LORD.

Psalm 116:3,4,13 (AMPC)

6- DREAMS VS. VISIONS & "WHO IS THAT DUDE?"

To you it was shown, that you might realize and have personal knowledge that the Lord is God; there is no other besides Him.

Deuteronomy 4:35 (AMPC)

It was late October and I hadn't told anyone about what happened and I didn't plan on telling anyone. My main concern was to figure out how I would survive the winter when I could barely walk or go up and down the stairs. How would I shovel the snow in this condition or even go down the driveway to get the mail.

On October 28th 2005 I was walking from my living room to the kitchen and I felt something very odd happening to my left leg. As I looked down panic struck me when I saw blood spurting out all over the rug and it was not stopping. It looked like a bad horror movie. The blood was thick and the color looked more orange than red. I sort of limped around the room to get my cell phone and I called 911, then I found my bag with my wallet and put my phone in there to bring with me. As I waited I thought about the coincidence of it being four years ago on October 28th that my mom passed away and it crossed my mind that I might be joining her soon, or she was making sure I didn't by forcing me to go to the hospital.

The town volunteer ambulance came and the police came and I can't remember who else but there were lots of people outside. By that time the bleeding had slowed so they bandaged the wound and prepped me for the ride. I couldn't walk so they brought me down the stairs strapped onto something like a wheelchair but without arms. When I was in the ambulance I couldn't breathe well lying down, so they let me sit up against the side of the ambulance. During the ride everyone was very nice to me and reassuring, but I was weirdly nonchalant, mostly apologetic for their inconvenience and for wearing my pajamas to the hospital. It was my usual frame of mind that I was unworthy somehow and did not want to bother anybody with my problems. I accepted whatever happened to me as a consequence of my own action or inaction.

When we arrived at the hospital it was time to lie back down on the stretcher and I heard everyone gasp as they pointed to what *appeared* to be at least a half gallon of my blood covering the back half of the ambulance floor. The pressure of me sitting up had caused the wound to continue to bleed out through the bandages. I found out much later the reason the blood looked orangey instead of red was because it was full of infection. It was indeed very yucky. I was wheeled to the waiting area and they elevated my leg and took all my information.

While I waited for the doctor to see me, the nurse on duty in the emergency room kept coming in and checking on me to see if I had passed out because she said, I was very quiet. What else was I supposed to do but wait? I did hear other people behind the curtain walls who were complaining and moving things around, but I think I was just happy that someone was going to help figure out what was going on in my body that was bad enough to make it burst open.

They took a blood sample and gave me fluids. When the doctor, who was actually a surgeon, came in and looked at my legs, he already knew from the discoloration and the wound what was going on. He told me and later confirmed I had Lymphedema. Basically, Lymphedema is a chronic condition where the protein rich fluid that remains after the body excretes waste, is not redistributed properly through the body and tends to collect in the extremities.

In my case there was an infection (resulting from the mosquito bite) which created an ulcer in the leg. He explained that it could possibly be taken care of as an outpatient, but he thought I was going to need surgery and that I most likely had this condition for a long time. He pushed out more of the infection, then treated and wrapped the leg in an Unna-boot which is a special dressing for this type of wound. He prescribed medications and told me if it was not getting better in five days, then I would need to have the surgery.

I was released with no way to get home except for a taxi-cab, but I could not fit into a cab bandaged the way I was, plus I was weak and in a fair amount of pain. The head nurse sat with me while I explained my situation of where I lived and she arranged for a special needs transport for me, which is like a private ambulance that I could pay for, to help me get back into my home. She waited with me the whole time and to my amazement, offered to come to my house one day with two other nurses and help me unpack my moving boxes. I was blown away by this gesture of kindness and the tears just began to flow. This woman was a stranger to me and had such a caring heart which I had not expected. As a matter of fact, not one person since my move here, treated me like I was too fat or lazy or just plain stupid for being in the condition I was in at the time. Sadly it was not the case with some other people I had known all my life. The nurse's name was Erica, and she encouraged me to get through this so I could be stronger and enjoy my new home.

During the next week I kept off my feet as much as I could and it so happened that my two sisters and their families drove up to see me for my birthday and to see my new home. I told them about my leg which they could see but I did not mention much of anything else; there was no point to bring it up. They stayed a few hours and unpacked some boxes to help me settle in better. When it was time to see the doctor again, I put a few essentials in a bag in case I would need the surgery and as it turned out, I didn't even make it to the appointment before the blood was leaking out form the bandages. I had to go straight to the hospital and would have the surgery that same day.

In all the preparation for surgery the surgeon discovered I was anemic and would need several blood transfusions before they could operate. He also said I was hypoxic which meant I was not getting enough air. The hypoxic condition would months later be diagnosed as C.O.P.D. causing me to need an oxygen concentrator to help me breathe 24 hrs. a day. Meanwhile, I was stable enough that I could have some anesthesia and proceed with the surgery. He briefly explained what to expect but I was not expecting the searing pain I felt during surgery. I was screaming as the anesthetist forcibly held down the mask on my face. I could hear myself screaming in pain that felt like burning knives stabbing into my legs over and over.

In the morning the surgeon came in to wake me and have a look at the leg. He asked how I was feeling and I told him about the stabbing pain I felt during the procedure. He chuckled and informed me, most patients don't remember that part. I let him know, "I FELT THE PAIN!" He gave as much anesthesia as he could do safely and explained that he cauterized the veins to stop the Lymphedema from creating new pathways and spreading out. He asked me if I knew I was septic and I looked at him puzzled. Did he mean like a septic tank for sewage? Eeeeww! He went on to explain, having septicemia is blood poisoning from an infection, which in my case started when I got that tiny mosquito bite on my leg and it got infected and traveled through my body. Combined with the Lymphedema and hypoxia and my body became inflamed and rotting from the inside out…..I found that *extremely gross* and at the same time I was thankful and happy to be getting treated, even if it was going to take a long time to heal, there was hope. I was extremely blessed that my leg exploded when it did or I would not be writing about it now.

On the first day after surgery they took off the bandages and told me I had to put my leg in a whirlpool bath and I thought they must surely be crazy. I had several open wounds which needed to be healed from the inside out, and had what looked like little drainage pipes of some sort that were sewn into my leg, so the yucky looking fluid would drain into the bandages, away from the healing wound. There was no way I was going to get up and stick my leg in hot swirling water! But... they made me do it...and it actually felt good. It was disgusting to see, like boiling raw meat, but it was necessary to get the wound on the way to healing. I went through that routine for a couple of weeks and I spent that Thanksgiving in the hospital and was thankful for a great many things as you might imagine. When I was finally able to be released, I was told to keep a very close watch on the wounds and to look for any signs that the infection might reappear.

A nurse was assigned to me and she would change the bandages because I wasn't strong enough to do that yet. It was really difficult to manage getting around the house to get food or get washed because I was still pretty weak and putting pressure on my other leg as I tried to walk with the help of a walker.

It was just weeks later when I woke up and my other leg had sprung a leak...more blood and infection and I was back in the hospital for more surgery and on Christmas Eve. I thought about the *coincidences* that both times I went by ambulance to the hospital were the same dates each of my parents had passed away.

While I waited in a room being prepped for surgery, I had my cane with me at my side when the attending nurse came in to start an IV fluid bag. He noticed it was a Sheleighly and I told him my Pop-Pop (grandfather) was born in Ireland and it was his cane. He told me his grandfather was born there too, in County Cork. Stunned I said, "So was mine, in County Cork, what year was he born?" He said "1888" and I said "Mine too, 1888!" Maybe they even each other! How is it possible that this nurse and I both happen to be here on Christmas Eve, to have this bond over an Irish cane? We laughed at the *coincidence* and chatted for a while longer.

By this time I knew these things were *not coincidence* and there was someone watching over me, assuring me that I was not alone. I wasn't sure who it was but I did know that God had to allow it, and it made me feel safe and hopeful. For this surgery they gave me a spinal block so I wouldn't feel the cauterizing, and I didn't. However, I did get to watch the operation and it was surreal to see the amount of bloody gobs of muck coming out of my own body. I lost over forty pounds through these two operations!

The infection in my blood caused a lot of damage and I was hoping this was the last of it but it wasn't. These open type wounds can take more than a year to heal properly because the cuts were inches deep into the leg and the inner layers have to slowly fit back together until the top layers meet and close the wound. My largest wound was over nine inches long by two inches deep and after it was more than halfway closed, there were signs that the infection was even deeper into the leg. So one more trip to the hospital and one more surgery, but this time was not as severe as the last two, and I was home again in a few days.

It took nearly two years before all five wounds were closed and the swelling was lessened, but the condition was ongoing because there is no cure for Lymphedema. I purchased a medical compression machine that looks like some kind of space suit for your legs, which if used daily keeps the fluid from building up. Then I just had to keep from getting cuts, scrapes, even bug bites, or an infection could start again. During that time I had help getting groceries and bandages or whatever I needed, but I was indoors with my legs elevated most of the time.

There really wasn't much time to meet neighbors before all this happened but that first winter we had a lot of snow and at least three separate times I woke up and saw someone had plowed my driveway. I couldn't imagine who did it because I didn't know anyone here yet. I thought maybe it was the company who delivered my fuel, so I called them and the woman told me it was most likely my neighbor who had a farm across the road. It wasn't till much later that I could fit my bandaged legs into my car and drive myself down the road a bit, so I was able to introduce myself and thank them for what they did for me. Once again, people who didn't even know me came to help me simply because they were good people. I was grateful to have moved to this town and I still feel that way because there are so many wonderful and genuinely caring people who live here.

During those first two years here I racked up quite a lot of bills from the hospital, homecare, medical supplies and other related expenses. While the hospital was kind enough to write off some of the expense to me, I had gone through all my savings because I no longer had insurance. Too much time had elapsed since my last job's extended insurance and I couldn't afford the high rates I would have to pay because of my condition. So I had many bills, no more money and I couldn't work. I could only stand for less than ten minutes at a time before I had to sit again from pain and swelling and sitting too long hurt my back. So that is how each day went, up, down, up, down, and it was exhausting just getting basic things done each day. I had to file a claim for my disability insurance benefits and fortunately my contribution through working all those years, was providing some relief to me now that I couldn't work. It wasn't much money but also it wasn't the first time I had to stretch a dollar, and I had become a pretty thrifty shopper. Only buy on sale and in bulk whenever possible.

Still having a great deal of pain in my legs especially around my knees, I eventually found a local doctor and would see him every couple of months so he could check my progress. He said I also had arthritis as well as the Lymphedema but ibuprofen would help with the pain. It did help a little. I used to love to walk for miles but that was not an option anymore and I felt like I really could use some exercise. I met a woman in the next town while I was shopping and we became friends. I told her I thought if I had a small pool I could exercise my legs like they did in the hospital and the water would take the pressure off my legs and joints. She helped me get one of those east set-up pools that have a top ring which you fill with air and then just fill the pool with water while it rises. As soon as I saw it filled I realized this is no different than my bathtub and I could not get up if I sat down that low. Eventually I found something I could use to step on to get in and pull myself up to get out.

So there I am one late afternoon, just feeling grateful and relaxed to be in this pool where my legs felt light as a feather. The sun had passed over my house and was behind some trees on my property. It was summer so all the trees were full except for the top of one tree that was dead so it just had naked branches. The sun was glowing a brilliant reddish orange color and hit those branches at such an angle that it looked to me as if they were on fire. It was really magnificent and I wished I had a camera handy. Then I squinted and it made it look even more so like it was burning. I said out loud, "Ha! It's like *the burning bush*, except that was full of life when the fire went away". I just kept watching and maybe ten, fifteen seconds later a swarm of birds came out of nowhere and landed on just those dead branches...which were now full of life! I was sort of in shock and wondered if I saw what I saw after what I said? There is really no one else around me to hear me, so I often talk out loud and now I had to wonder if I might be crazy or did someone...hear me? I said "God is that You?...Did You do that?" And I found myself laughing at the thought of God having a bit of fun up there. When I finally came to my senses and got out of the pool I started to walk and came across a big white feather. Just the one feather and it was not the color of the birds from the tree. I don't know if it was an Angel or God but I felt good about whatever it was...like I was not on my own anymore...someone was here.

It wasn't long after that when another odd thing happened. One morning I was still in bed and had what I thought was a lucid dream. It was happening in the spiritual realm so it was like a real-time vision that I could see while my eyes were still closed. Next to my bed is a window with lots of trees outside like a small forest. I saw a misty light come from the forest area through the window and alongside my bed. Then there came a petite woman maybe four foot tall, with straight dark hair that just grazed her shoulder and she walked deliberately slow on the path of light to the midpoint of my bed. She turned to face the bed and then raised her hand and passed it through the air over my body. I continued to watch in wonderment as she slowly moved her hand toward my mouth and nose, but as she got too close I got frightened and my whole body jerked awake! I sat up and grabbed the covers around me and tried to understand what just happened. I knew this...Angel?...Spirit?...must have come from the Lord, but I had not experienced anything like that before. It freaked me out a bit! Was it a warning? Was it a healing prayer? I was so disturbed by it that I pleaded out loud for whomever it was not to scare me like that again. The more I thought about it, I felt sure it was something good and then I felt sorry and ungrateful. Still freaked out, I apologized for reacting the way that I did, adding that it would be OK, if they wanted to come back again. I did see her again, but not for several years and I think it was because I was still fearful and untrusting. I had been through too many things in my life that took away my confidence and while I was definitely in need of all kinds of healing, it was going to be quite a while before I started to understand these subtle changes were drawing me closer to God.

O You Who hear prayer, to You shall all flesh come

Psalm 65:2 (AMPC)

Now that my wounds on my legs had closed it was a little easier to maneuver around, but since Lymphedema is a chronic condition with no cure, I still always had swelling and discoloration plus pain, some of which came from arthritis in the knees. It's hard to concentrate on much of anything if you're always in pain. I felt kind of useless to do something productive, especially since I was still having breathing difficulty even during minimal activity. Although the infection in my blood was gone, I had a long way to go and found that all I seemed to be able to do was eat, watch TV, send an email or two, eat, sleep, and repeat.

One morning in March I woke up and sat up on the edge of my bed and then I heard a distinct voice in my head say the name of an old friend of mine. For the purposes of this book I will pretend his name is Simon Strange. I wondered why his name popped into my head because I had not talked to him in almost ten years. I laughed out loud and then I heard the voice again saying "***Simon Strange***"! I continued to sit there puzzled because I heard the voice in my head but it seemed to be coming from the upper corner of the room, as if someone was there but I couldn't see them. I wondered if it was one of those weird things like, he passed away and was saying goodbye from the great beyond, which at the time was my impression of what happens to us after dying. Then as I was about to dismiss the whole thing and go on about my day, I heard the voice say once more, "***Simon Strange***"! Now I knew something was up for sure, because I was thinking one thought to myself at the same time I heard the voice speaking the name to me. I was starting to connect the dots so to speak. I've found many times in my life, if I come across something out of the ordinary, three times in a row, it usually turns out to be significant and I should pay attention. So I knew there was a mystery as to why I was hearing the name of *Simon Strange* that way. Especially since anyone who knew him personally, just called him Strange. This caused me not to dismiss it as a random thought in my head. I decided to look him up on the web, figuring if there was something major regarding him, I'd find it.

Simon Strange is someone I've known since I was sixteen years old. We all grew up in the same neighborhood where his friend was the boyfriend of my lifelong friend. Strange was an odd guy, but in a very good and creative way...*most* of the time. He was the kind of person that stood out in a crowd even though that was not his intention. He was over 6 ft tall, ruggedly handsome but sometimes goofy looking, intelligent but unassuming with a twisted but childlike sense of humor and all at the same time.

He had what seemed like unlimited energy and creativity. Simon Strange could build interestingly odd or complicated things from scratch or out of what ever materials he had on hand whether it was a musical instrument or a boat. He could draw, paint, write and he could debate a variety of topics just for fun. He would play devils advocate just to argue a point to death which he could care less about, if it would challenge or alter your perception of reality. I always thought, "This guy is so talented, if only he would use this power for doing good deeds instead of evil!" Although, one summer in the late 1970's, he started (without permission) painting a mystical mural on a school wall. By the time he had it partially sketched out, he had half the neighborhood including local cops, bringing him paint and brush donations and volunteering to help. The local reporters even showed up and wrote an article for the paper. It was stunning to look at as it wrapped around several walls of the school. What a shock it was to the students who returned to school only to walk through doors that had become part of a mystic mountain complete with wizards and gnomes. To some people he was cryptic, weird, overbearing, and or crazy. To me he was, well...all of those things plus he was cute, fun, and he was one of the very few people who accepted me for me. I accepted him for him too, because hanging around with Strange, was usually an adventure in itself.

Halloween seemed to be one of Strange's favorite holidays and at the first Halloween party I can remember, he built his costume and went as a human body part that randomly shot whipped cream out of its head. Sure there were times when he annoyed me or really pissed me off but, for the most part I had fun whenever I spent time with him which as the years went on, turned out to be less and less. I am more of a home-based person and he was a perpetual wanderer. Simon Strange loved to meet new people, try anything out of the ordinary, immersed himself in all manners of deviant-sub-counterculture, and had a following or a clique of sorts which included two of his best-est friends who I will call Missy and Quacky. Wherever one went, most likely all of them went. They did stuff like tour with the Grateful Dead or hang around with eclectic scientists and surfers who wrote code for NASA. Not your everyday sort of people unless they *were* your sort of people.

I think the last time I saw Simon Strange was around 1995, at of course, a Halloween party. Oddly enough he wasn't wearing a costume that year. I remember during that party we both had the same thought at different times and we wound up in the guest room to take a pause from the crowd. We had a great long talk about life and the future. I knew I learned something that night which was, if you are attracted to someone, or maybe love that they behave a certain way, then don't try to change them or make them fit into your plans, because then you risk changing the very things about them that attracted you in the first place. If you were to clip a rare bird's wings either to admire or keep it near and safe, you would take away the beauty of its grace as it flies free, and seeing just how high it can soar. I think the Holy Spirit led me to that understanding because that night was the last time I saw Mr. Strange, until I heard that voice and found him years later on the internet.

My first search turned up a bunch of articles and I could see that he had kept pretty busy and appeared to stay true to himself by the strange animated characters he created or fabulous artwork or projects he sold to major corporations. He also wrote some short fiction stories which were published in a compilation of that style of writing. So it seemed he did well and carved a niche in the wacky artistic community to which he was accustomed. I was happy to see that he was not dead and that he found success at just being himself. I printed some of the articles and put them in a folder as a keepsake and that was that. Or so I thought.

About three months later, my best and lifelong friend drove up for a visit. I'll call her by a nickname, Granada, having to do with the name of a car that was around when I first met her. We had both moved several times over the years and it was a long drive upstate from Long Island where she lived.

Even though it was rare that we saw each other in person, it felt like no time elapsed once we got together. She is the kind of friend that's laughing and telling a story even before she's got one foot out of the car. We crack ourselves up and especially after a couple of glasses of wine we could amuse ourselves for hours with memories of our dumb escapades and antics, which we surely would deny in public. As we were talking about who knows what, I remembered Simon Strange, and I told her about the voice I heard and how I found some information online about our mutual friend. She read the articles and said "Let's call him!" I told her I didn't think we should bother him after all this time and he would think we were crawling out of the woodwork because he became successful. She didn't think so at all and convinced me he was probably the same crazy guy we had always known and so we emailed him through one of his websites.

I emailed a basic hello from the two of us, wondering where he was living these days and that we found him on the web, but not mentioning how I *heard* the voice. It was the next morning when I received a new email from someone I didn't recognize. It was from **EGNARTS**, in bold caps which immediately drew my attention. I stared for a second and called to Granada, "Look, it's **STRANGE** spelled backwards!" That would definitely be typical of Mr. Strange to do, so already laughing, we read the email and it felt like an adventure had begun. Within minutes we were e-chatting back and forth and then traded phone numbers. As it turned out he had a house not too far from our old neighborhood and his close friends also had apartments there. We did some catching up and found that he had several friends within a few miles of where I now lived in Upstate NY. As a matter of fact he was driving up later that summer for a small festival that his friends held every year. Was this another *coincidence?* I purposely moved all the way Upstate where I didn't know a soul, only to find a connection to someone I already knew. *Strange* indeed I thought, but it felt good to be in contact with my old friend again and we kept up the emails several times a week.

I began to feel more energetic than I had been and in a better frame of mind, which caused me to pick up a pen and start writing poetry again and I had not done that in a very, very long time. I emailed a poem or two to him and he seemed to think they were good but maybe he just wanted to give me encouragement. We found that we still had some of the same interests and hobbies in common which among others included music, astronomy, science, politics, reading up on culture, spirituality and religious beliefs and also writing.

One day we were talking about some of the awesome photos taken by the Mars Rover, when he brought up that he had recently finished a science fiction based manuscript which he wrote for middle graders, and he asked if I had an interest in reading it and maybe provide some feedback. Of course I did! It's not as if I had a busy schedule other than sleeping, eating and some physical therapy. So he sent it to me in a few days and I let him know I intended to be brutally honest with my comments because it wouldn't do either of us any good otherwise.

I began to read page after page and aside from grammar issues and the fact that it was over 600 pages long, I was amazed at how well this detailed and historically accurate story, developed into a movie quality fantasy which hosted quirky and endearing characters. As I kept reading, I could just about see the whole thing play out in my head. When I was done, I told him which parts were my favorites and how much I loved the unique characters and the way he wove fascinating bits of history into the whole story. I also had to comment on the icky grammar, some redundancy and the long, very drawn out, lengthiness of the six-hundred plus pages of the entire story. (Yes, you're right…Who am I to point that out?) At that point he told me, he had a friend in publishing who read it and pretty much said the same things as I mentioned. Then he wondered if I might help with the editing and chopping down the length without losing the integrity of the story. I was surprised but really happy to do it. He let me know there was no rush and he just wanted to see if it would be good enough to publish. I already knew it was that good. I used to think my only talent was that I could see other people's talent even when they couldn't.

Now I had something I could work on to take my focus off my aches and pains and using a wireless keyboard, I could elevate my feet if need be and work from bed at my own pace. When you've worked hard all your life, it's not an easy adjustment to become inactive, whether it's due to illness or just retirement. This project was a blessing in disguise because it sparked that fire in my soul which had nearly gone out. I was feeling useful again and during that time I also kept up my poetry writing and wrote notes on dreams which I seemed to be having more often than not.

No person can ever really know what is in someone else's mind, but I knew Strange well enough to be able to figure what he would consider necessary to tell the story and keep his writing style intact. I would revamp a section at a time and we'd email back and forth or I should say we e-bickered, because that was the nature of our relationship for as long as I had known him. We agreed on a multitude of things, but there were always a few areas where we were polar opposites and as we were both equally stubborn, the only option we could agree on was to disagree. It must have been quite amusing to witness some of our absurd bickering over something so trivial, as if a fan should be turned on or off. Still, it was the kind of thing we could joke about because we knew we'd always remain friends. All in all I had a great time working with him on this project and at one point I realized the prediction made by the woman reading the tarot cards years earlier had come to pass! I had a relationship with someone I was working for, who I already knew, which brought me great joy. So at that time, I accepted the prophecy as fulfilled, and thought there really must be something to this horoscope and tarot stuff.

It took close to six months for us to finalize all changes and get the manuscript formatted to send out to publishers. Once that process was started, it was just a matter of waiting for replies. Time flies when you're having fun, but not when you are waiting, waiting, waiting, unless you occupy that time with other projects.

Somewhere in between working on the manuscript and doing my own writing, I got involved with some people in my community and we formed an environmental group. We were concerned about industrial projects that were supposed to come to our area, which is mostly rural and farmland. We investigated thoroughly and found these projects would have been extremely harmful, especially to our water supply. As a result, our group began to take steps to legally prevent greediness for profit and power, from overtaking our right to clean water and clean air, by exposing us and our land to toxic chemicals and other risky situations. Now that I was putting time and energy into all these things, I had new hope for my future. I often prayed and thanked God for these opportunities, to be of help to someone, instead of worrying about myself and my illnesses.

In this group I found many wonderfully caring individuals and we remain good friends. I made a promise to the Lord, that I would never take any money that was promised to us if we participated in helping these corporations develop their supposedly safe business in our area. There was a chance that they could actually use our land without our permission, and pay us a monetary pittance in return. I set up a website and put as much information about the business and its toxic process, and damage that had already taken place in other areas as a direct result of it. I posted photos and legal papers, links to other sites and anything else our group could find to help our battle. I did this with my dial-up speed computer! Fortunately, working years in customer service, I had developed a lot of patience. We had a big challenge ahead of us to find information we could use to fight against the deep pockets of big corporations. I felt sure that God must be helping us through all of this because I was having some very spiritually uplifting dreams and visions.

I have had flying dreams several times in my life and they are considered good, freeing dreams about escaping stressful situations or rising above the pressures of life. So it made sense to me that I would have this type of dream given certain negative situations over the years. Most of the flying I did was outdoors and as high or as fast as I wanted to go, but I could fly indoors as well. Once I dreamt I was flying in our basement and told my younger sister that she could fly too. Another time my dream took place in a school gym and I wanted to help the children learn how they could fly. However, when I asked other people who had these dreams to describe the position of their body as they flew, I didn't understand why nobody appeared to be flying in a position similar to mine. Either they flew like a super hero with a cape, meaning hands stretched out in front and the body horizontal in the air, or with their hands and feet dangling behind them as if there was an invisible rope around their waist pulling them upward. Try an image search for flying dreams on the web and you'll see what I mean.

In every one of my flying dreams, I was always flying feet first, as if power in my feet lifted them up and forward until my body looked like I could be sitting back in a recliner chair. That is how I always flew until more recently during this string of spiritual dreams when something incredible appeared to me. There I was flying in my reclined, feet first position, high up in the mountains on a perfectly sunny day. When all of a sudden, I saw a tall brick building on the mountain up ahead and I said, "I don't think I can make it over that!" As the words were still coming out of my mouth, I could see huge cumulus clouds forming up ahead to my left. These clouds were the most luminous white I had ever seen and dense as cauliflower. If you've ever seen a time lapsed video of cumulus clouds forming, that is how fast these appeared in the super bright sunlight. They began to take on the well defined form of a massive warrior-like arm. First the brawny shoulder down to the narrow elbow where it bent, then the muscular forearm to the wrist tied with bands, and then the hand of this mighty arm formed and swooped underneath me, lifting me up and over the building and all the mountains. I wish it went on from there but that's when I woke and sat there dumbfounded at having experienced this vivid dream.

I had to call my younger sister and tell her about it. When I did, she said, "Well I've heard people speak about the arm of God sometimes". That's when it really clicked for me and I realized that I always flew in that seated position, because God had me in the palm of His hand all the while, and He wanted me to know that. Now I knew for sure these dreams were happening for a reason...but why now and what's coming next? Not too long after that dream came another one but this was more intense and longer in duration.

I am calling it a vision because I was being spoken to while being shown different scenes of sorts. Where as in the cloud dream I could see all around me in detail, in this vision there seemed to be no walls, only hazy areas in which the scenes played out. I was just there, and then there was a person standing with me at my side. He was a man and wore light colored clothing but I didn't notice details and couldn't really see His face. I remember most of what He said, and I should have written everything down a soon as it was over but I didn't. I only realized later how important it is, to keep a journal of these things as they occur, to reference later.

One of the things He spoke to me was regarding Simon Strange, which I remembered but didn't understand. He also told me "***There is still time***" and showed me someone receiving Holy Communion. As I watched the scene, my Catholic training kicked in and I turned to Him saying, "Oh, I...I'm not worthy". Slowly, He turned and seemed to glide away and upward, as if on an escalator in a mall, until I couldn't see Him anymore. I immediately thought it's like the *Stairway to Heaven*! I knew this was something very real happening, something from God. But was it an Angel, a Spirit, or who was this Dude in my dream showing me these things? The first thing I did was to email Strange, and tell him what was said pertaining to him, and ask if there was any significance. Strange said he didn't have a clue what it meant, and he was having odd dreams himself, so I was still trying to make sense of everything

I was told. I did strongly sense I would need to find a local church and crack open one of the Bibles I had acquired over the years, though rarely if ever opened them to read scripture.

7- HE MEETS YOU WHERE YOU ARE

And the Lord said to Satan, From where did you come? Then Satan answered the Lord, From going to and fro on the earth and from walking up and down on it. Job 1:7 (AMPC)

It was kind of funny when my friend Strange, first told me he studied religion as a hobby, because I had always been curious about things of a spiritual nature. He also travels all over the planet meeting new people, so we had plenty of discussions about cultures and their different spiritual beliefs. One summer we went with friends to an outdoor Mormon festival in Palmyra NY. We watched a reenactment of how their founder Joseph Smith, brought their branch of Christianity into existence in the 1800's. There were also lectures, videos, and all things Mormon. After the play, the cast went into the audience to greet and answer any questions and hopefully sign up new members. I had a good time watching the play but no desire to sign up for anything. Everyone was very friendly and one member gave us a copy of the Mormon Bible, called 'The Book of Mormon'. I found it weirdly interesting but I didn't take it as truth or accurate, because there was something inside me that did not readily accept all of what they were preaching. When I later learned more about their "golden plates" and "magic stones" it seemed at least partially contrived. I believe the Holy Spirit was moving me along on my journey. Plus there were memories of my Catholic upbringing, which put the fear of God in me about the day of reckoning, by what it says at the end of the Book of Revelation.

I, Jesus, have sent My messenger (angel) to you to witness and to give you assurance of these things for the churches (assemblies). I am the Root (the Source) and the Offspring of David, the radiant and brilliant Morning Star. I [personally solemnly] warn everyone who listens to the statements of the prophecy [the predictions and the consolations and admonitions pertaining to them] in this book: If anyone shall add anything to them, God will add and lay upon him the plagues (the afflictions and the calamities) that are recorded and described in this book. And if anyone cancels or takes away from the statements of the book of this prophecy [these predictions relating to Christ's kingdom and its speedy triumph, together with the

consolations and admonitions or warnings pertaining to them], God will cancel and take away from him his share in the tree of life and in the city of holiness (purity and hallowedness), which are described and promised in this book. Revelation 22:16-18 (AMPC)

Now, while the reference is meant for 'The Book of Revelation', in my opinion, it might as well be for the whole 'Holy Bible'. In other words, let the Bible interpret the Bible and don't mess with it's content, or imply it needs a sequel.

The Mormons use the 'Holy Bible' and the 'Book of Mormon' which uses much of the scripture of the Bible, but removes or replaces content with conflicting material, containing the testimony of Joseph Smith, along with other witnesses, calling it scripture from ancient Americans. All in all I believe Mormons, to be good and loving Christians and God knows their hearts are toward Him. At that time in my life knowing as little as I did about the Word of God, but thanks be to Him, it was enough to keep me headed where I was being led and not get further sidetracked.

After the Mormon experience, I resumed my regular day to day activities and nothing out of the ordinary happened for a little while. Then I had a dream, or several dreams of the same nature. I kept seeing people who had passed away and were moving along. These were people I knew, like my grandmother and my mother walking along the road up ahead of me through fields of flowers and they waved happily and kept going ahead. There were dreams of my friends who had passed on, or of my friend's relatives who also passed and were in a waiting room of some sort, which seemed to be in my house. They were all trying to be helpful and reorganize my things so I could get rid of things that were not useful. I tried to let them know I didn't need their help, but they were not listening to me, they just kept throwing things out, and then a door opened, and I looked outside into the starry sky but I was afraid to go through the door.

Another dream was of an old friend who was supposed to be coming soon to visit, so I was getting ready, getting washed in the shower. Then I heard a loud knocking at the door, and I was frightened by the sound because I was not expecting this friend to be here this soon.

When I had these dreams I would usually think I had figured them out to some degree. I knew the dreams were from a higher source but, I just didn't know how much higher the source was in reality. I thought they were most likely friendly messages of love or warning, either for me, or the other people in my life. Are you able to connect the dots yet? (Old things pass away, letting go of the past and things which are no longer useful, doors opening, getting ready by washing in the water, a Friend coming soon, knocking at the door) Anyone who reads and has an understanding of the Bible would have recognized all those dreams have scriptural meaning, but I had only a vague idea of what was happening in my life.

I was feeling all sorts of happy about having the dreams, even if I had yet to figure out that God was trying to get my attention through the symbolism in these dreams. At least they were not the kind I used to have which were very dark and disturbing. There would be a few more dreams of the darker nature I was going to have to get through in the near future. However, by that time I was learning from the Teacher, how to put on my spiritual armor to fight and win against those attacks.

Meantime I had been emailing pretty much daily with Simon Strange, not just about the dreams, but news, politics, weather and where he had been traveling lately or his latest project. He had been in San Francisco, visiting friends and he shared pictures of a famous old boat which he previously helped rebuild and give it an update with his cryptic and brightly colored art painted inside and out.

He had also started writing a series of fictitious short stories, supposedly occurring on the old boat, which was written in the form of a continuous captain's log. Since we worked so well together getting his other book ready, bouncing ideas back and forth and pulling the weeds out of the garden so to speak, he asked me to read through these stories as well. However there was no garden in this series of stories, unless it was a garden of evil, which *only* grew weeds. These stories were in the same genre with H.P. Lovecraft, or Algernon Blackwood and very different from the more celestial book he had just written. I used to read this type of material so it didn't seem to bother me. I was interested in what he was writing, happy to help proof-read, and even took some of his suggestions to pick up used copies of books by the other authors I mentioned. In reading those stories, I had conflicting emotions. In the past, I really liked to read scary books or see scary movies, but now I wondered if my friend hadn't brought them to my attention, would I have chosen to read them? To my surprise, my answer was no.

On another occasion when Strange came up to visit, we went to his friend's summer festival and were talking about books in general, when someone mentioned an old used bookstore off one of the country roads. We decided to take a ride later and have a look around. It was just an old farmhouse on a dirt road, complete with rocking chair porch and squeaky screen door. There was also a small structure about a hundred yards away, about the size of an old outhouse or tool shed, which was filled with books that were two for a quarter or ten for a dollar.

Considering the price, my budget, and that I didn't want to climb the porch stairs, I decided to browse in the little old shed. My cane and I barely fit in there having not quite room enough to bend and see the books on the lower shelves. It was also hot and dark in this tiny space, so I had to leave the door propped open for light.

I reached up to touch the first eye-level shelf, where the first book I saw was written by the author, John C. Lily. He was famous for his work with dolphins, sensory deprivation tanks, and was also a friend of my friend, Simon Strange! He laughed later when I showed him what I found. What an odd coincidence to find something immediately familiar in such an out of the way place. Then I saw some plain brown books wrapped in plastic. I pull them down to read what they were about. They were old, brown and the title was, 'A Guide to Church Planting'. I wondered how that might happen; do you dig a hole, toss in a brick, bury it and pray for it to grow? I took those books because I thought the title was weird and it cost ten cents.

I was getting overheated in that space, so I quickly took a look on the adjacent wall, where my eyes stopped at a thick old red book sticking out from the rest. Aha! It was a Bible. I took it down, flipped through it and felt I should take this too, and it was ten cents! Next to where I found the Bible I took down another thick book which was a guide to writing your own book. "Interesting" I thought, because in the back of my mind I thought I would like to write a book someday. Having helped Strange with his book, gave me some actual experience and for the price of ten cents, I also took that book.

Then as I tried get out of there before I melted, I kicked (accidentally) a pile of books and saw a big book of 'Down Home Cooking' recipes. I love to cook for people and could not resist adding it to my other picks. I was almost out the door when I saw a small section of paperbacks that all had to do with "enlightenment". So, to make it an even dollar's worth of books, I took those as well.

As I felt then and I still feel now, those books were meant for me to find. What I didn't see then, but now I can see, is they represented choices of my past, present and future. I brought those home and added them to my piles of "to read" books, except for the red Bible, which I put near my bed.

It wasn't too long after that day, when I saw reports of a natural disaster on the news. I think it was the Samoan tsunami around 2010. When those things happen, and as we watch the reports of devastation and loss of life, like most people, I feel it in my gut and wonder how to help. Even if it were closer to where I lived, it's not likely I could be of much help, in my physical condition. What could I give financially, while I wasn't working, had my own pile of medical bills and was barely making it month to month? But the urge to give *something* was overwhelming. All I had in my bank account was about ten dollars. If that was all I had then I wanted to make sure it counted for something. There are many organizations out there that claim they are providing relief to the victims, but funds can get misdirected or misappropriated. So I went in search of the old preacher my mother used to watch on TV. When I found the Christian broadcasting network, I browsed though the titles for his name. I saw a few names I recognized but not his. Then I saw, 'Enjoying Everyday Life'. 'OK', I thought, "I could use a little enjoyment!" I waited for the show to start and the woman, Joyce Meyer, started talking about the "religiosity" of some Christians, and how it was more important to have a relationship with Christ, than to follow all the rules. In just a few minutes of listening, I knew this woman was speaking the truth. Not because it was what I wanted to hear, but because I could feel the words she spoke, as if they were already in my own spirit. Certain things just resonate in agreement within your being. I thought this was someone I could actually enjoy watching and hearing what she had to say. I looked her up online to see if she was *worthy of my whole ten bucks*. I found information on her organization and read the annual reports and independent audits. I was impressed with everything I read, and saw exactly how her outreach missions were providing both tangible and spiritual aid and love to those in need. It was more than enough proof for me to send my tiny ten dollars.

Because of what I learned from her teaching, eventually I was able to increase my contributions and know someone was receiving help. I continued to watch her broadcasts and they became part of my daily routine. I knew it couldn't be a coincidence that I found this show. It was very encouraging and something very different from the way I previously viewed religion. It made me want to read from the Bible, instead of just knowing I had one in the house *in case of emergency*. I started by reading the passages that Joyce made reference to in her broadcasts and little by little, I was getting a better understanding of Biblical things as they apply to our daily lives. I knew I wanted more of this in my life.

I began to look for used copies of her books which were all I could afford, but ordered a couple that seemed on target for where I was at that point in my life. One of the books was a 365-page devotional, which I learned is a, "daily dose" or "page a day" kind of book. One scripture, one explanation, one encouraging comment, and it all fit on about one page. I loved that idea! That was doable because I still had lots of questions and wondered how far was I going to go in this new direction? Bibles, books, TV shows, was there more to come down the road? Oh...yes, there was more and I still needed to find a church. For now though, I thought I would just continue to watch Joyce and keep listening to what she had to teach. Why had I never heard of this woman before? I found she was well known and at that time had nearly one hundred books published, and up till that time I didn't know she existed. I would later tell people about her and say "I never even heard of her 'till I heard of her". Only much, much, later did I realize that I sort of knew who she was.

There was a live comedy show I started watching back in the 1970's on Saturday night's. Yup, that's the one. One of the popular skits was about a *church lady*, who gave little sermons on how to steer clear of Satan. It was pretty funny but even funnier was, it could have been based on the woman who I am now blessed to hear, and who is surely anointed to teach God's Word.

Around that time I started to feel as if I had too many things going on, which was accented by how tired and achy I felt most of the time. I tried to keep perspective and think about what was important to me or my purpose, only to find out I didn't have a solid answer as to what my purpose might be in this life. God gives answers to many of our questions, even those questions we don't know how to ask, because He knows our heart. However, His answers come according to His timing and when we're ready to know how to handle the information. (And that's a good thing and a blessing.) The only thing to do was keep going and see what happens next. The next happening didn't take very long to get there.

For many years I read my horoscope every day. I did it for fun mostly, and there seems to be a bit of truth to characteristics of each zodiac sign. I have had several people close to me in my life either born on the same day or very close to the day, and they all had similar personalities and traits. I figured if their horoscope advised disagreements were in the air, I could avoid getting into an argument that day. I didn't run my life by it or take it all that seriously, but if that day's horoscope said blatantly, "do not fly on a plane today!" I don't think I would. And it could have turned out that a plane somewhere did have some kind of emergency or maybe not, but I thought at least it could be used as a guideline that made some sense.

I had the daily horoscopes and tarot readings on my computer's home page, along with news, comics, calendars, and assorted things of interest. One night I was sleeping in a bed that's in my guest/computer/storage room. I had a vision of my computer screen filled with rows and rows of faced down tarot cards. Slowly and one at a time they began to light up around the cards edge, so as to highlight the whole card. Then they began to light up faster and faster till they were just rapidly blinking on and off and then all at once they swirled up and disappeared, leaving three cards. There was one large card in the middle and two smaller cards. The large card lit up and an Angel appeared and spoke. I didn't understand the language, but the Angel spoke either a long name or a short sentence and disappeared. Then a smaller Angel appeared, spoke, disappeared and then the third Angel did the same. I still don't know if they spoke their names, or maybe prayer words, but the next day, I had no desire to read my horoscope. I felt like I wasn't supposed to be reading predictions and I wasn't really sure why. Within the next few days, I decided to remove the horoscopes, tarot cards, and pretty much every other distraction on my computer's home page. I never looked back or questioned if that was the right thing to do, because I knew it was coming from a higher source.

Not long after that day I had another dream, a vision of something handed down from someone above me. In the dream, it seemed someone was teaching me by showing me three wooden stick figures and one stick figure with a white dress on it. The three were placed one above the other, so three in a row up and down. The figure in the white, which looked like a bridal dress, was standing next to the third figure at the bottom. Continuing in the dream I thought, "Oh, is that my grandfather, father, and…?...new husband?" I took the bridal figure and moved it from the side to the front of the bottom stick figure so they were face to face, the way little children face their dolls to do *kissy kissy*. Then the teacher took the bridal figure from me and moved it back to the side of the bottom figure. I felt confused and sorry and said, "Oh, OK". Still not knowing this was the real Teacher, as in the Holy Spirit, was explaining the relationship of Father, Son-(Groom) and Holy Spirit, and the Church-(Bride). Then I said, "Mom, Is that you?" I reached my hand up in the air and said, "If you're there, please, can you just touch my hand?" I waited in the silence for what seemed a very a long time and eventually something touched my hand and I was awake. While I had faith enough to believe in God's existence, my mind was not yet ready to believe that He is more than willing to speak to us. He met me at my level of faith, where *I could believe* a loved one was speaking to me.

Even though He let me hold on to that comfort for a while, one day as I was thinking of her, He showed me my mother was resting and she looked so serene. By that time my faith had grown enough to understand, the Holy Spirit was teaching me. Something else I realized later was the use of stick figures in my dream. While both my sisters have ability to draw, I did not and the only things I could draw were stick figures and trees. So that was another example of the Lord using what is uniquely familiar to us to reach and teach us.

Once again I found myself thinking about all the dreams and messages and wondering, should I be doing something more? I knew it was time to find a church and partake in Holy Communion, as I was shown in the vision. I didn't want to go to the Catholic Church in town because I still had unresolved issues from what I was taught growing up.

I decided to go to the Presbyterian Church, because some people from our community environmental group were members of that Church and let us have meetings in their dinning room. Through that connection, I met one of the Church Elders and he was always so friendly and cheerful, so I thought I would start there. I found out at that first Sunday service, there were similarities and differences between Catholics and Presbyterians.

One such difference being Catholics, kneel during parts of Mass and Presbyterians do not kneel during any part of service. Presbyterians partake of Holy Communion once each month on the first Sunday, as apposed to the Catholics who partake on every Sunday or Saturday at minimum. As it happened, I was there on a non-Communion week.

Another difference was Presbyterians don't have confessional booths where you tell the Priest your sins, nor do they have Priests, they have Pastors. They confess as a group during the silent confession part of the service, or in private on their own time spent in prayer. Fortunately for me, (seriously, I had decades of sin to unburden from my soul!) I learned from reading and listening to Joyce Meyer's preaching, and later getting confirmation in the Bible, that it is acceptable to God, if we take this more direct approach to confession.

I acknowledged my sin to You, and my iniquity I did not hide. I said, I will confess my transgressions to the Lord [continually unfolding the past till all is told]— then You [instantly] forgave me the guilt and iniquity of my sin. Selah [pause, and calmly think of that]! Psalm 32:5 (AMPC)

When we accept Jesus Christ as our Savior, and from our heart confess our sins to the Father, even in private, we have forgiveness through the sacrifice of the Son, which was sufficient payment in full, for all past, present, and future sins of the believer. Believe me when I say, no matter what's on your sin list, if it's been a long time coming, when you finally have that serious conversation with God, the tears will flow until you are empty, but you will feel His love for you and be filled with hope.

I continued to go to that same Church each week, until it was the first Sunday of the next month and I was excited to finally receive Communion as I had been shown. Guess what? OK, I'll tell you. It seems the people who had been preaching at the services were members of that or another Church, but none were actual Pastors. Nobody told me they had been without a Pastor for many months, and without a Pastor, they do not practice Holy Communion. Hmmmm….Now what do I do? Well, I continued to go there anyway, praying in hopes they would soon have a new Pastor, or until I thought of something else.

Meanwhile I continued to receive lots of inspiration through listening to Joyce on TV, reading her other books and of course, my Bible. I noticed that several times she made reference to the Amplified Bible she was using. I kept thinking what is that? Is it a book on tape? (This is what we called audio books in the 70's & 80's, instead of e-books, mp3's etc...) Finally she explained it and it was not a recording of any sort. I understood it to be the Holy Bible, with words (in parenthesis) which add further explanation or context, so the scripture can be correctly understood by the reader.

So they read from the Book of the Law of God distinctly, faithfully amplifying and giving the sense so that [the people] understood the reading.   Nehemiah 8:8 (AMPC)

So if a sentence of a book read: *The boy went to buy what was needed.* The amplified sentence might read: *The boy went (on a donkey to town) to buy what was needed. (Sacks of flour for the ceremony)*

Even if that sentence was taken out of its original (book) context, with the amplified sentence, we would still know for example, the boy did not go to a local pawn shop to buy a gun.

This is doubly good because many people quote scripture out of context to make a point, but have improper understanding of its true meaning. That only spreads confusion. I remember hearing a certain celebrity on a reality type game show, who quoted the scripture, "Vengeance is mine, saith the Lord!" She was using this to justify getting back at someone who wronged her. If kept in context or amplified, we see the real meaning which is, vengeance does not belong to us and it does only belong to the Lord.

Beloved, never avenge yourselves, but leave the way open for [God's] wrath; for it is written, Vengeance is Mine, I will repay (requite), says the Lord   Romans 12:19 (AMPC)

I decided I wanted a copy of the Amplified Bible and looked online finding there were several choices. I also found that Joyce Meyer, was given permission (no easy task) to make a specialty Bible, (after years of teaching) containing the Amplified Bible, along with her own teaching notes and so much more. Maybe it's sounding like Joyce is my idol, but it is God who anointed her to do this work. It becomes evident if you spend any time hearing her preach God's Word, and she always points back to Him. So I put her particular version, called 'The Everyday Life Bible' on my Christmas list and got it the following year. Yippee! Now I actually love and will not do without reading the Bible. I have such a deeper understanding through the amplified version which was the shock to my system I desperately needed. For all of you musically inclined, the **amp**lified, would be the electrified or plugged-in version.

As the weeks went on, I continued studying and learning about how God uses all the things that have happened in our lives to redirect us toward Him.

Accepting Christ as our Savior means we are born again, and have the Holy Spirit living in us. He wants to guide us and have a relationship with us throughout our lives. He speaks to us through other people, or dreams and visions, just like what was happening to me. But, when I found out He speaks in that *still small voice* to our mind and sometimes audibly, that was a revelation for me.

"Huh?... You mean, *that still small voice* is not just a metaphor?... Not just a gut feeing of right and wrong? I don't remember ever being taught quite like that. So...that Dude in my dreams?.....that was God speaking to me in the Spirit! Wow..., Oh!..... Uhmmm, Lord, I'm so sorry I referred to You as Dude...hope that was not a sin, but I thank You for the forgiveness right about now."

This was really good news and beyond exciting, to think that our Lord would want to communicate with us as we live through each day.

I had a lot to think about and I began to trace back all the *weird coincidences* that brought me to where I was now. Suddenly all my dreams and visions had become clear signs to me that we have a true and living God. The struggling in my life to go against the flow of society and seek solitude was not without a purpose after all. I didn't move here to die in peace, I moved here to get born again! I was what you would call a baby Christian, and I was learning that a lot of me still had to die, (old habits) and make room for Christ to live in me as I live in

Him. I had become a new creature in Christ and that would take some getting used to because I thought I would have to change all at once. Thanks be to God, for He is patient!

Over the years my tastes, styles and interests have remained pretty consistent. I'm referring to my own nature, personality and inner self, as opposed to whatever is trending in the world. I'm of the opinion, change is necessary for growth, but not all change is necessary and not all change is growth. I found the more time I spent trying to adapt myself to someone else's idea of whom I should be or what I should be doing, the less I liked myself. And there was that same questioning inside me, just as I had questions about religion, I questioned what's wrong with taking time to know who I was supposed to become in this world? But where does that time come from when you're busy trying to keep up with other people's expectations of what you're supposed to achieve?

When I thought about it, I felt there was something I was purposed to do and I always seemed to be close to the surface but not able to break through and see what it was. I needed direction but didn't have enough trust in anybody's advice. I like simple, but appreciate intricate design that makes it seem that way. I am in awe of nature's stunning beauty, but also of its Divine craftsmanship. I love music & poetry and how uncomplicated notes or words, flow out of and tap deep into our souls and emotions. I like mysteries and how science can be applied to solve them, yet some things are meant to remain inexplicable or enigmatic. I like learning about different cultures and seeing that our appearances are different but we all have the same needs. Beyond basics of shelter, food and water, we need love and acceptance, forgiveness and guidance, so we can be happy and prosperous. Then we need to give those very things to others, because you can not be truly prosperous and happy without sharing what is tangible and what is spiritual. Some of us spend our lives searching for these things, only to find poor imitations and never feel satisfied. We seek enlightenment to find the true meaning of life and what our purpose might be. We ask how to live in this chaotic secular world, so we look for wisdom and answers by consulting a variety of seemingly higher and more knowledgeable sources including scientific law.

There is enough of what seems like truth or fact in these curious tools that might unlock the mysteries of life. We might put our faith or trust in horoscopes, mediums, tarot cards, I-Ching, philosophers, even scientific theory, etc...However, over time all things including facts can change, until only truth remains. And well intentioned as it seems to be, the knowledge or wisdom we get is at best partial truth, like pieces to an endless puzzle, and at worst complete deception. Satan will use these avenues to deceive you into accepting a lesser version of your life, instead of the blessings which God has ordained for you through a life in Jesus Christ.

There shall not be found among you anyone who makes his son or daughter pass through the fire, or who uses divination, or is a soothsayer, or an augur, or a sorcerer,

Or a charmer, or a medium, or a wizard, or a necromancer.

For all who do these things are an abomination to the Lord, and it is because of these abominable practices that the Lord your God is driving them out before you.

The Lord your God will raise up for you a prophet (Prophet) from the midst of your brethren like me [Moses]; to him you shall listen. Deuteronomy 18:10-12,15

How sad, that by my relationship with Simon Strange, I readily accepted the reading from the woman with the tarot cards as prophesy being fulfilled. I had no understanding back then, of God's heart toward us and desire for us to have a relationship with Him. All the while, the Lord had much greater plans to fill my life with joy.

Be well balanced (temperate, sober of mind), be vigilant and cautious at all times; for that enemy of yours, the devil, roams around like a lion roaring [in fierce hunger], seeking someone to seize upon and devour.   1 Peter 5:8 (AMPC)

Just as bad, some of us consider ourselves independent, relying on our own savvy and intellect to figure things out or get us where we want to go in life. Some believe only in what can be explained or proven scientifically. Without a Christ centered life, all other sources are faulty or false gods, providing temporary comfort and flawed solutions. There can only be one God who is the Truth and source of all Life. Why not go right to the source?

For it was in Him that all things were created, in heaven and on earth, things seen and things unseen, whether thrones, dominions, rulers, or authorities; all things were created and exist through Him [by His service, intervention] and in and for Him. And He Himself existed before all things, and in Him all things consist (cohere, are held together).   Colossians 1:16-17 (AMPC)

Your absolute best life will be built on the solid Rock of Salvation.

My soul, wait only upon God and silently submit to Him; for my hope and expectation are from Him.

He only is my Rock and my Salvation; He is my Defense and my Fortress, I shall not be moved.   Psalm 62:5-6 (AMPC)

Like the song title from those British boys suggests, "All You Need is Love". I happen to agree with that title because, I know God is love and He is all I need to rely on in life. True wisdom will always point to Him.

But the wisdom from above is first of all pure (undefiled); then it is peace-loving, courteous (considerate, gentle). [It is willing to] yield to reason, full of compassion and good fruits; it is wholehearted and straightforward, impartial and unfeigned (free from doubts, wavering, and insincerity). James 3:17 (AMPC)

Even before we know how to seek Him, we can see signs that He is here with us, to lead us to a better life on earth than we could ever have without Him. And in the end…Love will call us home to eternal life.

God finds us where we are hiding. Many people use phrases like, *when you find God*, or *she found God*, as if He was hiding from us. We are the ones who are lost or hiding, not Him. He is here with us showing us the Way we should be going by whatever will get our attention and change our direction to where He leads. He happened to find me in my dreams, through music, movies, friends, even my computer, because He knows our hearts and what we need. It is God's Perfect System…GPS…always ready to recalculate your route if you make a wrong turn. He meets you where you are.

8- DENOMINATIONS & OBLIGATIONS VS. GALATIANS

(Denominations are for money not Christians)

But if you show servile regard (prejudice, favoritism) for people, you commit sin and are rebuked and convicted by the Law as violators and offenders.

For whosoever keeps the Law [as a] whole but stumbles and offends in one [single instance] has become guilty of [breaking] all of it.

For He Who said, You shall not commit adultery, also said, You shall not kill. If you do not commit adultery but do kill, you have become guilty of transgressing the [whole] Law.

James 2:9-11 (AMPC

My sisters have told me through the years, they think I might be more spiritually connected to the other side than some other people. That's not the case at all. We all have the ability to hear God's voice, because just like a recipe calls for a pinch of salt, He put the ability to hear His voice in us as a *measure of faith*. But you have to choose to activate your faith. In other words, He sent you the link, but clicking on it is your choice. Whether you go to church regularly or not at all, if you don't know what it is to be led by the Spirit or to hear His voice, but you would like to have that happen in your life, then just ask Him plainly in prayer, to help you know Him, in whatever way will best get your attention.

"And whatever you ask for in prayer, believing, you will receive." Matthew 21:22 (AMPC)

I also don't think of it as the other side, because He is here with us and He is actively reaching out with His love for us. It's like another realm that exists alongside us right now. With me perhaps, since I have always had an interest in nature, science, or mysterious things in general, I devoted more time to those things in solitude. Much like camping out and seeing the stars at night without the distraction of city lights; they look like shimmering diamonds on black velvet. If you're in a quiet space without distractions or noise to drown it out, it's hard to miss that *knock at the door* or that *still small voice*. Even so, it took me almost half my life to know and understand *Who* was speaking to me. The next time I heard from God, it was the middle of winter. It was the night before Christmas, to be exact. The Presbyterian Church still had no Pastor and I was determined to receive Holy Communion on this Holy Day of Obligation. So I set out to go to the Catholic Church which was just a few miles from my home. Physically, I was still having trouble walking, driving and even breathing in the cold weather. This night however, was frigid, icy, snowy, and the handicap parking spots in the lot were all filled. I parked as close as I could but it was a long way for me and I was out of breath by the time I got to the door. Unfamiliar with the layout of the Church, I opened the door to find I was at the wrong entrance and I wound up in the Clergy's changing room. I had to exit and walk around the entire building to the front door. Still freezing and trying to breathe calmly, I opened the door. I could see it was obligatorily jam packed, absolutely no seats, with people crowded together right up to the doorway. I could only stand for minutes at a time before it was too painful and I had to get off my feet. Then tears fell, stinging my frozen cheeks as I started back to my car.

Once inside my car I just sat with a blanket and cried. I kept thinking in my head, it's a holy day of obligation and I failed. I really wanted to receive Communion but I couldn't do it. Still crying, I prayed to God and said I was sorry I failed again and I went on explaining about, no Pastor and the bad weather and no room at the Church. (As if He wouldn't understand my situation on this particular eve....I can only imagine Mary at nine months pregnant riding that donkey through the desert!)

And when I got quiet, I heard, "**Galatians 2:20**".

"What???" "Galatians 2:20? Galatians 2:20, Galatians 2:20".

I repeated it several times so I wouldn't forget it, but questioning; "Did I really just hear that?" I knew it wasn't my own voice because I had no idea what that was, other than I knew it was in the Bible. When I was a little kid I thought Galatians had to do with Gladiators, but now I was sure the Lord just spoke to me! "I am not crazy, I am not crazy, and I am not crazy, Galatians, 2:20" I thought, as I sat there a little longer just incase there was more. Then I said; "I thank You Lord and I love You Lord, Amen".

Driving home, I kept wondering what Galatians was about. Was I in trouble? Will I get a do-over? I had reverential fear of God, so I was a little nervous at what I might find, ya' know what I mean? So I headed for the Bible near my bed and found the passage. I read Galatians 2:20 and 21 because that was the end of that section.

I have been crucified with Christ [in Him I have shared His crucifixion]; it is no longer I who live, but Christ (the Messiah) lives in me; and the life I now live in the body I live by faith in (by adherence to and reliance on and complete trust in) the Son of God, Who loved me and gave Himself up for me.

[Therefore, I do not treat God's gracious gift as something of minor importance and defeat its very purpose] I do not set
aside and invalidate and frustrate and nullify the grace (unmerited favor) of God. For if justification (righteousness, acquittal from guilt) comes through [observing the ritual of] the Law, then Christ (the Messiah) died groundlessly and to no purpose and in vain. [His death was then wholly superfluous.]
Galatians 2:20-21(AMPC)

I've used the amplified classic version here, but the version I had at that time actually used the word "obligation" in the notations when describing, observing ritual of the law. I knew once again, the Lord heard my prayer, saw my tears, and cared to give me great comfort, even as I failed. I never said the word obligation out loud, but it was in my head as my old Catholic auto-response. Catholics call certain religious holidays, Holy Days of Obligation. That's legalism, calling attention to the Law.

I read Galatians over and over and even looked up definitions to be sure about what I was reading. Clearly the Lord was letting me know, if we are believers in Christ, we are made righteous **by what He accomplished** through His Crucifixion and Resurrection, and **not by anything we do**, or don't do, or by the observance of rituals or keeping of the law. He doesn't love us only when we do good things, He loves us no matter what because *He* is good.

God is not keeping score of things we did wrong, but encourages and enables us to do good. Would you tell your toddlers how many times they fell down before they were able to walk? Or would you help them up and just be happy they kept trying and celebrate their progress? To feel guilty because I did not attend church on that day would mean I did not understand the gift of freedom that Christ died to give me. Does that mean I will no longer go to church, even on specific holidays, or confess to Him when I sin? Not at all, but I will live joyfully by faith and do these things from my heart, which is in Him, not because the church requires me to do so. God is pleased with us because He is pleased with Christ and we are in Him and He is in us. That means even if we step out and fail, or even when we don't deserve it, He shows us mercy and gives us grace, so we can continue to grow and try again.

To live by faith means to trust the Lord and rely only on His guidance, through His Word. He will always lead you to the people, places and things, which will benefit you more than you could know or ever expect. So, I began to read and study all of Galatians and it's without a doubt, still my favorite book of the Bible. There is so much freedom that comes from reading just that one Book of the Bible. It reveals why Grace is amazing and how the Truth sets you free. Christianity, would not exist without Christ, yet so many denominations of the Christian Church, continue to focus mainly on preaching rules of their doctrine, rather than focusing on, Who we are in Christ and the personal relationship He desires to have with us.

For I know the plans and thoughts that I have for you,' says the LORD, 'plans for peace and well-being and not for disaster to give you a future and a hope. Jeremiah 29:11(AMPC)

We are His Church and we can be beacons in this world, whether it's in our physical Church or in our day to day lives. We each have a part in His plan, but how can we know that great plan if we don't even know how to hear from Him? Not only can the Lord fix what is broken in our lives but He will lead us to our best joyful life, then our light will be a reflection of Jesus. He will not ever leave us without support to get where we need to be.

If we do not understand what it really means when we say "In Christ", then we and our Church will stay as slaves, stuck in the past and not able to break forth and grow. The Bible contains the Old Testament (Old Covenant) and the New Testament (New Covenant). While it is advantageous to read and know the whole Bible, it is wise to adhere to the New Covenant which God gave us through the Blood of Christ. We are living in the end times of the New Testament. If we do a little comparison of what God's Word says in our Bible, to the doctrines of any Christian denomination, we find various adaptations with conflicting judgmental rules and regulations that dictate; when we go to church, who can go, who is not welcomed. Some dictate which sins are forgiven, who can give or receive Communion, how often, and who is excluded. Others tell us who gets baptized and when, or follow rituals of what, when, and how much to eat or drink. There are various religious titles with authority to preach, teach or lead. Ideas of who can marry and who can not, or about tithing being required (giving 10% of your earnings) or optional. Some tell when to stand, sit, kneel, what to wear, how long to pray, and who to pray to and for what reason etc...— That's exhausting!

How can we all be Christians and have so much confusion about what that means? How do we become one Church united in Christ?

Well, first (and last) we need to know the Truth, because that comes from God. The in-between confusion came from us through many years of being prideful, not so perfect yet humans, trying to adapt

God's plan for us as we see fit for our generation and circumstance, rather than let God adapt us through the Spirit to fit His plan. However, we are Christians and have the advantage of The Holy Bible containing the Word of God, which does not change. What Jesus spoke concerning us, is there for all to read, along with the testimony of those who heard directly from Him and also the Holy Spirit. We can learn from the vantage points of Matthew, Mark, Luke and John, who together give us the gospel of Jesus Christ.

As we said before, so I now say again: If anyone is preaching to you a gospel different from or contrary to that which you received [from us], let him be accursed (anathema, devoted to destruction, doomed to eternal punishment)!

For I want you to know, brethren, that the Gospel which was proclaimed and made known by me is not man's gospel [a human invention, according to or patterned after any human standard].

For indeed I did not receive it from man, nor was I taught it, but [it came to me] through a [direct] revelation [given] by Jesus Christ (the Messiah). Galatians 1:9, 11-12 (AMPC)

We can eliminate judgmental behavior and

discrimination between denominations and all believers in Christ, and know we have been forgiven and blessed. There are a great many Churches that are Christ centered, thriving and have caring outreach programs, but there are also many Churches with dwindling congregations. The difference is where there is legalism, there is lack, and where there is forgiveness there is freedom to flourish. By that I don't mean to say there should be no sense of order and leadership in the Church. People need direction to know which way to go, but Jesus said "I am the Way". Jesus did not focus on people's sin and failures and turn away from them. He welcomed sinners, forgave them, set them free, healed them and made them strong and prosperous.

Like newborn babies you should crave (thirst for, earnestly desire) the pure (unadulterated) spiritual milk, that by it you may be nurtured and grow unto [completed] salvation, Since you have [already] tasted the goodness and kindness of the Lord.   1Peter2:2-3 (AMPC)

That is what a Church should be for people, a place for unconditional love, acceptance, forgiveness, healing, and building up, not discrimination or condemnation of any sort. We've all sinned but have all been made righteous according to how God views the believer. Our sins were covered in the blood of Christ, so God does not see them anymore. I wouldn't want to go to a Church every week to be reminded of how much I screwed up. That would be depressing! How can we grow without proper nourishment? We need inspired preaching and we need to read the Word for ourselves and know the encouragement it brings to our lives.

Having moved several times over the years I know of Christian Churches that denied families or certain people attendance because they did not have or give enough money, their children were disobedient or their clothes too dirty, they were gay or lesbian, they drank wine, enjoyed dancing, sang non traditional songs of worship, or they had no written proof of being baptized. *Whether these are sins or not is irrelevant to how we treat people*, because accepting Jesus Christ as Lord and Savior means *we are forgiven* all of our sins through that relationship.

If the Church is Christ centered then the doors must be open to all who would seek Him, without judgment and with love.

God hates sin, but loves the sinner, and if there are sinful behaviors in our lives that need to be changed, that can only happen through the work of The Holy Spirit within us. He will direct and set the pace of our steps.

But the fruit of the [Holy] Spirit [the work which His presence within accomplishes] is love, joy (gladness), peace, patience (an even temper, forbearance), kindness, goodness (benevolence), faithfulness, Gentleness (meekness, humility), self-control (self-restraint, continence). Against such things there is no law [that can bring a charge]. Galatians 5:22-23 (AMPC)

Just to make a point here though, let's look at drinking wine which some of the Church believes is sinful and the same goes for dancing.

Jesus' first miracle was turning water into wine. Mother Mary and Jesus were invited to a wedding and at one point the wine ran out, so Mary asked Jesus to help out. He told the servants to fill six, twenty- thirty gallon containers with water and then He did that miracle thing which we all love so much and turned all that water into wine...really good wine at that! That's a lot of gallons of wine and there was probably dancing during the event. We know Jesus never sinned and He would never lead someone to sin, so how can drinking wine or dancing be a sin? The Bible tells us in several places, not to be a *drunkard* or be given to drink *much* wine.

In like manner the deacons [must be] worthy of respect, not shifty and double-talkers but sincere in what they say, not given to much wine, not greedy for base gain [craving wealth and resorting to ignoble and dishonest methods of getting it]. 1Timothy 3:8

But that is very different from saying not to drink at all, because God's word is intentional.

And when the manager tasted the water just now turned into wine, not knowing where it came from— though the servants who had drawn the water knew— he called the bridegroom

And said to him, Everyone else serves his best wine first, and when people have drunk freely, then he serves that which is not so good; but you have kept back the good wine until now!

This, the first of His signs (miracles, wonderworks), Jesus performed in Cana of Galilee, and manifested His glory [by it He displayed His greatness and His power openly], and His disciples believed in Him [adhered to, trusted in, and relied on Him]. John 2:9-11 (AMPC)

For John came neither eating nor drinking [with others], and they say, He has a demon! The Son of Man came eating and drinking [with others], and they say, Behold, a glutton and a wine drinker, a friend of tax collectors and [especially wicked] sinners! Yet wisdom is justified and vindicated by what she does (her deeds) and by her children. Matthew 11:18-19 (AMPC)

And as for dancing....

Let them praise His name in chorus and choir and with the [single or group] dance; let them sing praises to Him with the tambourine and lyre! Psalm 149:3 (AMPC)

A time to weep and a time to laugh, a time to mourn and a time to dance, Ecclesiastes 3;4 (AMPC)

The Bible does however tell us that *if we believe* it is sinful, *then for us* to do it would be sin (even if the Lord would not think it is sinful) because we did it while believing in our hearts it was sin. The Lord knows our hearts.

But the man who has doubts (misgivings, an uneasy conscience) about eating, and then eats [perhaps because of you], stands condemned [before God], because he is not true to his convictions and he does not act from faith. For whatever does not originate and proceed from faith is sin [whatever is done without a conviction of its approval by God is sinful]. Romans 14:23 (AMPC)

Now getting back to Galatians and why it is so important to know who we are in Christ.

Galatians was a letter from Paul to the Churches of Galatia. Who was Paul? Saul of Tarsus (not to be confused with, King Saul the first King of Israel) was a Pharisee, who was a devout observer of Jewish tradition and The Law. He actually persecuted Christians, even approved the stoning of the Apostle Stephen, and wanted all followers destroyed. He thought he was doing this for God and did not believe the crucified Jesus was the Messiah. Then one day on the road to Damascus, Jesus appeared to him and basically said *Hey Saul, why on earth are you coming after Me by persecuting my followers?*

Saul was blinded by The Lord's great light and cried for three days begging forgiveness.

Now as he traveled on, he came near to Damascus, and suddenly a light from heaven flashed around him, And he fell to the ground. Then he heard a voice saying to him, Saul, Saul, why are you persecuting Me [harassing, troubling, and molesting Me]?And Saul said, Who are You, Lord? And He said, I am Jesus, Whom you are persecuting. It is dangerous and it will turn out badly for you to keep kicking against the goad [to offer vain and perilous resistance]. Trembling and

astonished he asked, Lord, what do You desire me to do? The Lord said to him, But arise and go into the city, and you will be told what you must do. Act9:3-6 (AMPC)

Then the Lord sent someone to restore his sight and he became know as Paul, and after being taught by the Holy Spirit for a few years, he went on to preach the Truth and actually wrote many of the books of the New Testament.

So you see Saul/Paul was the absolute worst kind of sinner, right? But Jesus, with unconditional love turned him from a Hell bound killer to a best selling writer of non-fiction. Really...The Holy Bible has sold more than any other book ever! Jesus can work miracles in your life too. In his letter to the churches of Galatia, Paul was reminding them of how they first became free of the curse of the law through Christ and warning not to live in the old ways of being under Jewish tradition and law, before they became followers of Jesus.

If we go to a school where they require us to wear a uniform, do we still wear the uniform after we graduate? No. If we meet up with people who have not graduated yet, do we put on the uniform again? Hopefully we do not, but if we do, Paul reminds us that we are free from the dreaded school uniform! Yippeee!

The Christians of Galatia seemed to be living just fine

until their old Jewish acquaintances showed up and then they turned back to Jewish tradition and rituals, so as to appear righteous to them, which was being double minded. This can also become a problem in the Christian churches today. We should be celebrating that Jesus Christ has set us free from the stress and burden of perfectly keeping the whole law.

For I will be merciful and gracious toward their sins and I will remember their deeds of unrighteousness no more. When God speaks of a new [covenant or agreement], He makes the first one obsolete (out of use). And what is obsolete (out of use and annulled because of age) is ripe for disappearance and to be dispensed with altogether.   Hebrews 8: 12-13 (AMPC)

We have been forgiven and should thankfully receive His healing love and strength. We as Christians are blessed and have access to all of God's resources through Christ, and we have the Holy Spirit to help guide us in using those resources not only for ourselves but to reach out and help all those in need.

Jesus gave us only two commands and told us by doing those two; the by-product would be that we have not broken the law which is lower than these two commands.

Teacher, which kind of commandment is great and important (the principal kind) in the Law? [Some commandments are light—which are heavy?] And He replied to him, You shall love the Lord your God with all your heart and with all your soul and with all your mind (intellect). This is the great (most important, principal) and first commandment. And a second is like it: You shall love your neighbor as [you do] yourself. These two commandments sum up and upon them depend all the Law and the Prophets. Matthew 26:36-40 (AMPC)

Yet there are so many Christian churches that focus and still preach on obedience to The Ten Commandments. They focus on faults and failures and what we should not do.

Adam had one commandment...and he could not keep from breaking it because Satan kept him conscious of the law, by directing his attention to the one thing he should not do.

God gave people the law because they wanted to know exactly what these sins were and because they thought they could obey God and be made righteous through keeping the Law.

The top ten were known as the Ten Commandments

but there were more than 600 other laws!! God knew people could never keep all the laws, and breaking even one law is as if all were broken. Breaking even a small piece off a perfectly whole plate means you have broken the whole plate. Without unblemished blood sacrifices to pay for forgiveness, all sin leads to the curse of eternal death. God told us from the beginning, in His promises to Abraham (Abraham's seed), He would send a Savior. God sent His Son, not to remove the law, but to once and for all people be sacrificed, by taking our punishment, so we as believers in Him are forgiven and saved. Jesus came to give us new life and brought us from the negative place of *(**Thou Shall Not**)* struggling to meet requirements of righteousness, to a positive place of (***You Shall***) being more than conquers as joint heirs to the Kingdom in Him.

Just this week as I am writing about this very thing, I was listening to one of the Christian radio stations and heard a preacher I had not heard of before. He was telling us to make our children read the Ten Commandments every night to the point of memorizing them because that is the only way they will know what is the wrong thing to do in life. He kept stressing the point of memorization, just as he had been taught as a boy. One again, here is the concern with that kind of teaching. If you keep focusing on what you should not be doing, then you are not focusing on what you should be doing and you won't grow because you can't focus on both. If we keep the focus on Jesus and what He told us to do, we will enjoy being fruitful Christians who are lead by the Spirit. Just as it was in Paul's day, so it still goes on today and this is why some Christian churches struggle while others thrive. The Old Testament is just that, OLD-Shall Not. the New Testament is the NEW-Shall way of living.

Do not [earnestly] remember the former things; neither consider the things of old. Behold, I am doing a new thing! Now it springs forth; do you not perceive and know it and will you not give heed to it? I will even make a way in the wilderness and rivers in the desert.   Isaiah 43:18-19 (AMPC)

It will make such a difference in every area of your life if you know how loved you are by God, and you can begin to know this through the right teaching, right believing and the reading the Word for yourself. Instead of being worried over denominations, rules and regulations we can be united in Christ, as we're told in Galatians.

For in Christ Jesus you are all sons of God through faith. For as many [of you] as were baptized into Christ [into a spiritual union and communion with Christ, the Anointed One, the Messiah] have put on (clothed yourselves with) Christ.

There is [now no distinction] neither Jew nor Greek, there is neither slave nor free, there is not male and female; for you are all one in Christ Jesus.

And if you belong to Christ [are in Him Who is Abraham's Seed], then you are Abraham's offspring and [spiritual] heirs according to promise. Galatians 3:26-29 (AMPC)

We tend to think; what about the sins of so and so, surely they're excluded from forgiveness...what they did was sinful right? Christ came to redeem sinners. Perfect people have no need to be redeemed, so every person including you and I, have need for mercy and forgiveness through Christ. Let's take for example the issue of being gay and Christian. As Christians, if we were to judge someone as sinful, then we too have sinned and condemn ourselves Believers in Christ have the full assurance that all of our sins are forgiven, even while we're being transformed. Jesus did not come to judge or punish He came to forgive, heal and love us and that is how we are to treat each other. We are each other's neighbor. God truly knows what is in our hearts, and we'll be judged on how well we shared His unconditional love with our neighbors. As we just read in Galatians, there's no more distinction between Jew and Greek, slave and free, male and female for those in Christ.

If Christ (the head), does not see gender distinction, then how can His Church (the body), see anything other than that we are all One in Christ. Knowing who we are in Christ gives us real strength and power to overcome any obstacles in life, whatever they may be. God's Word tells us that we are being *transformed* into His image as we continue our journey in Christ. Even though we do make mistakes, we have already been forgiven and should not live as hypocrites and condemn ourselves or others. Knowing God loves us and does not condemn us means we can live in harmony with love for God, ourselves and others. God sent Jesus and said audibly, **"This is my Son in whom I am well pleased"** If we are in Christ, then God is also pleased with us while we are being transformed, because of that relationship.

For we were not following cleverly devised stories when we made known to you the power and coming of our Lord Jesus Christ (the Messiah), but we were eyewitnesses of His majesty (grandeur, authority of sovereign power).

For when He was invested with honor and glory from God the Father and a voice was borne to Him by the [splendid] Majestic Glory [in the bright cloud that overshadowed Him, saying], This is My beloved Son in Whom I am well pleased and delight,

We [actually] heard this voice borne out of heaven, for we were together with Him on the holy mountain.

2Peter1:16-18(AMPC)

To clarify the relationship further:

Jesus said to him, I am the Way and the Truth and the Life; no one comes to the Father except by (through) Me. John 14:6 (AMPC)

I'm not sure why some Christian denominations are partial to preaching laws of the Old Testament and I do not question that they believe what they preach is good for their Church. Perhaps they think we might forget that sinful behavior leads to pain and suffering in our lives so they keep reminding us of our sin. But condemnation and guilt also brings stress causing sickness, disease, pain and suffering.

I know from my own experience, when I was told I was a sinner and a failure, I felt worthless; I still sinned and still failed and eventually nearly died. When I was told I was forgiven and loved, I could forgive and I could love and it wasn't in my heart to sin anymore and it brought healing both physically and spiritually.

I do know it is alright for us to question if what we are hearing is the Truth, as long as we are not judging those who are doing good in Jesus' name. As Christians, no matter what denomination we choose, we can exercise our personal faith, by looking to Jesus and letting the Holy Spirit be our Guide.

John said to Him, Teacher, we saw a man who does not

follow along with us driving out demons in Your name, and we forbade him to do it, because he is not one of our band [of Your disciples].

But Jesus said, Do not restrain or hinder or forbid him; for no one who does a mighty work in My name will soon afterward be able to speak evil of Me.

For he who is not against us is for us. For I tell you truly, whoever gives you a cup of water to drink because you belong to and bear the name of Christ will by no means fail to get his reward. Mark 9:38-41 (AMPC)

Reading Galatians set me free from my old way of thinking and brought new perspective to the meaning of being a Christian. I had a new found curiosity with every book, chapter, and verse I read in the Bible and found who I am in Christ. The following verse from 2 Corinthians also corroborates what Galatians reveals about the Holy Spirit living in us.

You show and make obvious that you are a letter from Christ delivered by us, not written with ink but with [the] Spirit of [the] living God, not on tablets of stone but on tablets of human hearts.

Such is the reliance and confidence that we have through Christ toward and with reference to God.

Not that we are fit (qualified and sufficient in ability) of ourselves to form personal judgments or to claim or count anything as coming from us, but our power and ability and sufficiency are from God.

[It is He] Who has qualified us [making us to be fit and worthy and sufficient] as ministers and dispensers of a new covenant [of salvation through Christ], not [ministers] of the letter (of legally written code) but of the Spirit; for the code [of the Law] kills, but the [Holy] Spirit makes alive.

2 Corinthians 3:3-6 (AMPC)

Here are a few more things I now know from my journey which applies to whosoever will believe in Christ as their Lord and Savior.

Have the roots [of your being] firmly and deeply planted [in Him, fixed and founded in Him], being continually built up in Him, becoming increasingly more confirmed and established in the faith, just as you were taught, and abounding and overflowing in it with thanksgiving. Colossians 2:7

In Him we have redemption (deliverance and salvation) through His blood, the remission (forgiveness) of our offenses (shortcomings and trespasses), in accordance with the riches and the generosity of His gracious favor. Ephesians 1:7

For we are God's [own] handiwork (His

workmanship), recreated in Christ Jesus, [born anew] that we may do those good works which God predestined (planned beforehand) for us [taking paths which He prepared ahead of time], that we should walk in them [living the good life which He prearranged and made ready for us to live].
Ephesians 2:10

You have been regenerated (born again), not from a mortal origin seed, sperm), but from one that is immortal by the ever living and lasting Word of God.
1 Peter 1:23

And God's peace [shall be yours, that tranquil state of a soul assured of its salvation through Christ, and so fearing nothing from God and being content with its earthly lot of whatever sort that is, that peace] which transcends all understanding shall garrison and mount guard over your hearts and minds in Christ Jesus.
Philippians 4:7

I have strength for all things in Christ Who empowers me [I am ready for anything and equal to anything through Him Who infuses inner strength into me; I am self-sufficient in Christ's sufficiency]. Philippians 4:13

And my God will liberally supply (fill to the full) your every need according to His riches in glory in Christ Jesus Philippians 4:19

9- COMMUNION, 3ʳᴅ DAY VISION & HEALING

[For it is He] Who delivered and saved us and called us with a calling in itself holy and leading to holiness [to a life of consecration, a vocation of holiness]; [He did it] not because of anything of merit that we have done, but because of and to further His own purpose and grace (unmerited favor) which was given us in Christ Jesus before the world began [eternal ages ago].

2 Timothy 1:9 (AMPC)

All through that winter I wasn't able to get out much because physically I didn't do very well in the frigid weather. It was hard to breathe and I wasn't steady on my feet in the mixed terrain of ice and snow on the hills. Even with snow tires and four wheel drive there were still times my car slid down the steeper icy inclines of the mountain. So I would stay put and had plenty of time for exploring my Bible, or books and shows by my new favorite evangelical, Joyce Meyer. This was something I never thought I would say, but I looked forward these things and was excited to keep learning more about my relationship with the Lord. It became evident to me that I was happier the more time I spent doing this, so I kept going.

Spring soon was on the way and my sister asked if I would come down to watch her house while she went on vacation with her husband and their two daughters. I felt strong enough to do that but it was a long drive and I wasn't so sure about that part. I knew I would have to stop several times and stretch my legs to keep the circulation going, but slowly and steadily I went. I prayed for protection before going. I asked the Lord if this is something I was able to do and then, to please keep watch over me and the other drivers while I made the trip. I had learned most of Psalm 91, which became one of my favorites and I use it often.

On that day I set out to my sister's house I prayed: "*He covers me with His wings and I am safe in His care, His faithfulness protects and defends me*", which is adapted from, Psalm 91:4

I repeated it a few times on the way, and no sooner did I get on the main highway, when right along side me was a huge tractor-trailer painted black with huge gold and white wings across and it read **Smith Transport**. Now it may seem like just a coincidence, but the road I started out on was **Smith Road**. Maybe that's part of ***"seek and you shall find" Luke 11:9.***

I did feel it was confirmation of His protection when I saw those well timed huge gold eagle wings. I arrived safely thanks be to God.

While I was at my sister's house, which happened to be Easter week, I debated in my head if I would be able to attend service at my sister's church, which was about a half hour drive. I wondered if it would it be over crowed because of the Holiday. I knew I couldn't stand up if there were no seats, and I didn't want to wind up sitting in the parking lot again but I really wanted to receive Communion.

As it happened, that Good Friday the phone rang as I was sitting right there, but let the answering machine take the call because with the family away, it's just easier than explaining that and then taking a message. I heard a woman's voice asking for my young niece, to see if she was available to help at church to make the flowered Easter Cross. I knew that was something that required a timely answer so I grabbed the phone. I explained the girls were on vacation and I was just watching the house. She said, "Oh that's too bad, but if you're not busy would you like to come down and help?" I explained about my condition, but said I would think about it and she gave me the directions and what time they would be there on Saturday.

At that point, I was unsure if I would go; even though I thought it might be nice to help I wondered if I went Saturday, would I have the energy to go to Church Sunday. I usually had to plan my daily activities with time in-between to rest and recover, as pathetic as that probably sounds it's true.

Meanwhile, my sister called to say thanks and wish me a Happy Easter. I mentioned the woman who called from church and I asked if the girls had done that flower thing before. She said no, and the woman had never called them for any reason in all the years they lived there. Once again, I felt this is not a coincidence that the church lady was calling for the first time ever and I was sitting right there to hear her request.

I decided I would go Saturday and help. I found the Church and the woman who I spoke to on the phone, and to my surprise she was limping and explained she had forgotten her cane. It just so happened I had an extra one in my car, so I brought it in for her to use. We talked as we sat there weaving flowers together for the parishioners to put on the Easter Cross on Sunday. It turned out that we had very similar stories about being sick and recovering with God's help. She had been through many surgeries and was now doing well and had a great attitude of faith. I believe God used this particular woman to lead me back to church and after spending the morning there meeting people and working together, I knew I would be able to come back for Easter Sunday service. It felt great to be of help to someone else but it was also helping me.

When I left there I started going over the prayers which I remembered from the Catholic mass, so I would be more prepared to participate in the Easter service. My sister's church was Episcopal, but they use similar prayers like,

Sanctus:

Holy, holy, holy Lord, God of power and might,
heaven and earth are full of your glory.
Hosanna in the highest.
Blessed is he who comes in the name of the Lord.
Hosanna in the highest.

If there's one thing about the Catholics, it's they're big on memorizing prayers. We were taught to repeat some prayers three times, as in, to the Father, Son and Holy Spirit. Recalling what I said to the Lord in my vision about being unworthy, I repeated three times, "Lord, I am not worthy to receive You, but only say the word and I shall be healed". At the time I wasn't thinking of the exact Bible story of why we said that before Communion but I knew it was significant to that Divine exchange.

Easter Sunday came and we had a beautiful service. I

sat near the back where there was more room for me to stretch out my legs and still be out of the way. There were two choirs and two pastors for this specially decorated service. There were also at least four others who helped during the Holy Communion, with real wine and bread. As the service went on, I became aware that more than any other time in my life; I felt a connection to every word being spoken. When it came time to receive Holy Communion, I was on the verge of tears because I knew this is what the Lord meant for me to do and I could feel His presence with me during that service. After I received the Body & Blood of Christ and said Amen, I went back to my seat and could not stop the tears. This experience for me was very cathartic and I knew I was meant to do more in this life. Now in Christ, I was on my way.

It was a little rainy that day and when I got back to my sister's house I went into the family room where there was a big skylight and I sat down to put my feet up and looked up through the skylight to see a rainbow just forming through the clouds. It was a very good and beautiful day to celebrate Christ has died, Christ has risen and Christ will come again, Amen.

Easter was Sunday and then Monday was just a low-key day for me, I was content to spend time with all the house pets. My sister and her husband not only have two daughters, they also have two rescue dogs and two cats and sometimes extra rescue critters that need forever homes. Seeing as I usually live alone with one cat, this was an adventure, just to keep track of and feed them all. But I had fun playing games or just sitting with them all lined up on the couch watching movies. Later, I went to bed and read a little from the Bible before sleeping.

As I woke early Tuesday morning, (which by the way was the *third day* after Easter morning) I heard a voice say **"Only say the word and I shall be healed, Only say the word and I shall be healed, Only say the word and I shall be healed"**. Then silence and then it was as if I was in a different space, sitting on a bench where there was another woman and a child next to me. I couldn't see any walls or ceiling but I felt like I was in a hospital waiting area. There was a long hallway to my left and a man came from that direction pushing a cart of some sort and walked over to me. He was extremely tall, like a giant and had dark brown hair and very large beautiful hazel eyes with really long eyelashes. He didn't speak but he looked at me, sat down next to me, bent down and seemed to touch my lower leg. At this same time I had the feeling or the impression that he was *looking for work* but I don't know why because he never spoke.

I remember thinking maybe I could help him find work because I thought he was mute. I called out "Wait!" just as he was getting up and walked slowly past me and then vanished along with the woman and child. It seemed without any time passing my attention was drawn upward to the sky. Then I could see something appearing from beyond the sky, and by that I mean it was not as if it was in the sky, but it was as if the sky opened and a huge curtain unrolled from that space. It was white and gold-ish in color with even a slight hue of sea-glass-green and it flowed in the breeze in slow motion like a flag, but this was altogether Holy in appearance. All of a sudden I could see a stage or an altar and the same tall man was there. I watched him speaking words that I couldn't hear while at the same time, he made signs with his hands. Then he took something from the cart and sprinkled it from his hand over me like a priest would do at a Baptism. I wanted to look up to see where the curtain came from but I could not look away from the beautiful eyes of this man. Just as I thought I would try to look up through the sky, everything faded and I was awake.

I hadn't had something so real happen to me since I had the vision of the Spirit that waked beside my bed. Yet, this was something more amazing and unforgettable and it was absolutely from God. I knew that I had finally obeyed what He showed me to do by receiving the Body and Blood of Christ on Easter morning, and on this third day, I believe He gave me a baptizing or healing blessing.

After my sister's family returned home, we talked about their trip and my flower weaving experience at their church. I didn't tell them about my vision till over a year later, because even though I had previously mentioned some of my dreams to my family, I don't think they were ready to hear that the Lord was speaking to me.

My sisters and I all grew up as Catholics who drifted from the Catholic Church, and they were familiar with my stumbling spiritual journey through things like astrology, mediums, and spiritual dreams, and they dabbled in their own ideas of spirituality, but I didn't think I would convince them that, *now* I am hearing from God!

When I was settled back at home again, I came across two other preachers who were similar in message to Joyce Meyer, but had their own styles of anointed preaching. The first was Joseph Prince, who explains the importance of right believing and breaks down biblical words by syllables from original languages of the Bible, to show the clear intention of God's Word. He offers proof that what is contained in the Bible is accurate and every scripture has a purpose for being written. I found this extremely helpful, especially when it came to understanding changes that were taking place in me and in my life. We serve a living God and having faith that His Word is true can mean the difference between just hoping good things will happen in your life, or knowing the power contained in God's Word can make miracles happen. Unfortunately many people are of the mindset, I'll believe it when I can see it, or when science says it can happen. But God is not a man...He is God, so it's more like, first you believe it then you receive it, in His impeccable timing. If we don't believe God will do a miracle in our lives, then why should He do it? We would look to give the credit to someone or something else which our minds could process. To have the kind of faith that produces miracles means, it is necessary to believe that God exists, is willing to do something and that His word is true.

And He reached out His hand and touched him, saying, I am willing; be cleansed by being cured. And instantly his leprosy was cured and cleansed. Matthew 8:3(AMPC)

So shall My word be that goes forth out of My mouth: it shall not return to Me void [without producing any effect, useless], but it shall accomplish that which I please and purpose, and it shall prosper in the thing for which I sent it. Isaiah 55:11(AMPC)

We can be armed with the knowledge that our living God, wants to help us and that His word is true and accurately recorded in the Bible. Whatever He spoke will be accomplished, so we can expect as believers in Christ, we are forgiven, loved, blessed, healed, cleansed, refreshed, renewed and prosperous. We didn't earn any of this because of anything we did, but we can expect it because of what Jesus did for us.

In Him we have redemption (deliverance and salvation) through His blood, the remission (forgiveness) of our offenses (shortcomings and trespasses), in accordance with the riches and the generosity of His gracious favor.   Ephesians 1:7 (AMPC)

We will see the manifestation of those good things as we keep believing and are being transformed and guided by the Holy Spirit. We are all at different points in our spiritual journey, so some will see things happen immediately, while others which is most of us, will see gradual progression as we learn to trust in and rely on the Lord, to make us ready to handle the blessings He wants to bring into our lives.

And we also [especially] thank God continually for this, that when you received the message of God [which you heard] from us, you welcomed it not as the word of [mere] men, but as it truly is, the Word of God, which is effectually at work in you who believe [exercising its superhuman power in those who adhere to and trust in and rely on it].   1 Thessalonians 2:13

And all the multitude were seeking to touch Him, for healing power was all the while going forth from Him

and curing them all [saving them from severe illnesses or calamities] Luke 6:19(AMPC)

I knew I wanted to be healed and healthy because it was in my heart to do good things and help people, but I had obstacles to be cleared out of my own life before being able to do many of those things. I also needed to receive those things from the Lord in order to be able to give help to others. I had been able to forgive everyone in my life for whatever wrong they had done to me because I saw what unforgiveness does to people. I no longer wanted to keep that inside me where it kept the hurt alive and feeding on my entire being. The Lord forgave me which in turn gave me the power to forgive. I let go of that part of my past but I still had to forgive myself which seemed harder. I had hurt people in my life and sometimes it was intentional and sometimes it was survival, but there were also times I wasn't even aware I hurt someone until much later. I had already confessed sorrow to the Lord for all my wrong doings which was more than I would like to admit, but you can't hide from God and I did feel better in my heart about many things.

There were several times when opportunity presented itself and the Holy Spirit gave me courage to ask forgiveness of certain people I had wronged in my life. Eventually I was able to understand forgiveness was also meant for me.

Aside from Joyce Meyer and Joseph Prince, I also like to hear the preaching of Joel Osteen. If you ever need a pick me up kind of message, then I can recommend Joel. I am usually in a good mood and consider myself a positive person, but we all have days when we just need a hug. Joel has an anointing to hug you with his sermons. Whatever downside you might be experiencing, He will make you see the flip side and even laugh at it. Whenever my mind felt like dwelling in the past, I found Joel Osteen's website or read from one of his books and always wound up smiling and refreshed.

Between Joyce, Joseph and Joel, I found a really strong alliance in Christ. Along with their personal testimonies and their ministries, they all make reference to the power of God's Word and how it is activated by reading it and speaking it for ourselves. It's great to hear anointed preaching, but as we grow in Christ we need to participate by doing as the Word says, if we want to see the great plan God has for us come to fruition.

When we say there is power in God's Word, it's not figurative like when a public figure or leader might give a powerful speech and we say it moved us or we were touched. In that instance it is our emotion which might cause us to take action because of what we heard, however there is no authority behind it as a guarantee that something will happen. With God's Word, there is a very real transference of energy when we speak it in faith and according to His will. He spoke the world into existence, which science likes to call the big bang, but actually illustrates the literal power of God's word, which does not return void, but does what it sets out to accomplish.

God the Father spoke though God the Son while He was still with us, and later through God the Holy Spirit sent by the resurrected Jesus Christ. When we become familiar with His Word and speak in faith according to His will over our lives, we bring God's power into our circumstance. If that sounds like three different sources of power it's not. We have One Triune God. Consider a fiber optic light for a minute. There is one source of light, which can appear as more than one light by fiber optic strands which allow us to see the light in another place. There is still only one source of the light and the strands of fiber only do as the light source does. If the light source got brighter or changed colors, then so would the light at the end of the fiber optic strands. Even if the light source was outside of our house and we let a fiber strand into our house through a cracked window, there would be light inside, from the outside source.

Once more Jesus addressed the crowd. He said, I am the Light of the world. He who follows Me will not be walking in the dark, but will have the Light which is Life   John 8:12 (AMPC)

Since the night I tried to take my life and told the Lord I could no longer take care of myself, He not only forgave me but he also started a healing process in me. I was born again as a new creature, a baby Christian with a new heart, needing love, nourishment and time to grow. I think He would have miraculously healed me in that moment, but I would have croaked from a heart attack in amazement. I am one of those people who receive gradual healing because although I do believe in miracles, my mind and spirit were not where they needed to be that they could believe my total healing. Even so, the Holy Spirit was leading me to grow my faith and prepare for gradual healing. Much like the wounds on my legs, I needed to be healed from the inside out. When I had a better understanding of the relationship between Father, Son and Holy Spirit, and who I am in Christ, I was able to understand what happened next.

It was only after I had the belief in God's Word as Truth, let go of my past, and obeyed what the Lord had shown me to do by receiving Holy Communion, that I saw His face in a vision. In previous visions I when I saw this Man or heard His voice, I could not quite see a face. As I mentioned before He meets us where we are and uses familiar things from our lives to reach us. With me it's often through song titles or lyrics, but this time He used TV shows and movies that were familiar to me. Early in the morning as I woke, I saw something like a window or frame or mirror, in it I saw the face of a young man from head to shoulder, probably thirty-ish. He had sort of strawberry blonde slightly tousled wavy hair down to the shoulder. He had fair skin and dark eyes, and He seemed to be smiling and said to me, "*I will teach you all you need to know*". A few seconds passed and He vanished. Immediately thoughts came into my mind that He looked like a cross between Ron Howard as *Opie Taylor,* from *The Andy Griffith Show* and the actor from *Mask*, Eric Stoltz. I associate those types with innocence or goodness. Then I also thought of the movie *Below*, where on a ship, a man looked into a mirror and saw himself at first, but then noticed it was the spirit of someone who was murdered that was looking back at him.

When I put together what all these images represented *to me personally;* the innocent person, killed, at first masking his appearance but then revealing he was a spirit, I knew this was indeed the Teacher, sent by God. I have no idea if that is really what the Father, Son or Holy Spirit looks like, but He used what was familiar to me, just as He will use what is familiar to you, because while God places no great importance on outward appearance, He is all things to all people. I remember seeing a painting done by a young girl who said she saw Jesus, and in her painting which was beautiful, He had dark hair, blue eyes and looked as if He just stepped out of a stylish hair salon.

I feel overly blessed that He would care enough at all to appear in my dreams or let me hear His voice and I pray that happens in your life as well. We will all truly see His Glory when He returns for us, which I hope will be soon. Meanwhile I will just continue where He leads.

Not long after that vision, there was another one. I saw myself reading the Bible. It was opened on my lap and as I held the sides, the top half of the pages became fluid, rippling like water and then sudden jolt of electrical current passed through it and I jumped. I felt the electricity. I mean that literally and I had to look around to see if I was near anything that would have caused that to happen. I believe the Lord showed this to me to punctuate there is active power in the Word of God.

I was thinking about all the visions I had been having and how much I was learning and I was really beginning to see how God was working in my life. But the revelation of speaking relevant scripture over our lives to bring the power of God into our circumstance, made me remember the importance of Holy Communion and the words we speak. At least in some Christian services, before Communion we say "Lord I am not worthy to receive you but only say the word and I shall be healed". Then we receive the Body and Blood of Christ (the wine and bread) which is given for us and we say, Amen. This comes from the Bible story of the Centurion who came to ask Jesus to heal his servant who was at home and ill. He felt that he was not worthy to have Jesus go all the way to his home, but he believed if Jesus would just say the word, then the far away servant would be healed.

But the centurion replied to Him, Lord, I am not worthy or fit to have You come under my roof; but only speak the word, and my servant boy will be cured

Then to the centurion Jesus said, Go; it shall be done for you as you have believed. And the servant boy was restored to health at that very moment. Matthew 8:8, 13 (AMPC)

As we speak the Word of God, believing it by faith during the transaction of Holy Communion, our faith releases His power so we can receive our healing which He promised.

For I will restore health to you, and I will heal your wounds, says the Lord… Jeremiah 3:17 (AMPC)

Back then the Centurion saw Jesus in person and knew that Jesus healed people. Today we know that *Jesus took our sins and sickness with Him when he was crucified*, but our physical bodies have to catch up by believing that truth in our mind. Something must first be believed possible in the mind, before it can become a physical reality. It's sort of like an inventor's mind has to believe in his own head that something is possible before he can create it in reality. So when we remember Jesus Christ by partaking His Body and Blood in Holy Communion, we are speaking in faith thereby releasing His healing power through that Divine exchange.

For the story and message of the cross is sheer absurdity and folly to those who are perishing and on their way to perdition, but to us who are being saved it is the [manifestation of] the power of God.

1 Corinthians 1:18 (AMPC)

Like the Centurion, as we believe we will receive. At that point in my journey, I did believe the vision I received on the third morning after Easter was because of my rebirth and renewed faith though Communion, and healing was now able to manifest in my life. Without noticeable change in how my legs felt, I had not really paid any attention to how they looked since that day. It was the revelation of power in the Word that caused me to look down at my legs. Due to the trauma and Lymphedema they remained blackened from the ankles to just below my knees for years after my surgery. Now I saw there was a clear spot right in the center of where the tall man in the vision bent to touch my leg. It was clearing from that mark most of the way up to the knee. It's as crazy as it sounds but that's the way it happened. The scars are still there, but I am Ok with that because they serve as a reminder of the loving God Who carries me in my weakness.

10- TESTING, TESTING, ONE, TWO, THREE

Let us all come forward and draw near with true (honest and sincere) hearts in unqualified assurance and absolute conviction engendered by faith (by that leaning of the entire human personality on God in absolute trust and confidence in His power, wisdom, and goodness), having our hearts sprinkled and purified from a guilty (evil) conscience and our bodies cleansed with pure water. Hebrews 10:22 (AMPC)

All through my years I believed in God, so I would pray once in a while, not so much for me but for the world and the things I would witness going on that seemed so horrific. You only have to take a glance at the news each day to see that evil is on the rampage with no plans to stop anytime soon. I figured just as my bad choices led to bad things in my life, that the evil and disasters in the world were a result of the world's combined sins. What I did not fully understand was God let evil loose in the world for a finite amount of time, but as believers we live under the Grace of God. Grace is God's mercy, loving kindness and favor toward us. His grace provides the means, to be protected from evil or come through what it brings into our lives and be made stronger, simply by trusting in our faithful Savior, Jesus Christ. Without understanding that our faith in Him is a shield, we might give in, give up, or try to attach blame to God, for what is evil in the world. God is not the author of chaos and destruction in the world. Satan the deceiver would like for you to believe that lie, but it is he who is responsible for the horrific spread of evil and destruction in the world.

But He said to me, My grace (My favor and loving-kindness and mercy) is enough for you [sufficient against any danger and enables you to bear the trouble manfully]; for My strength and power are made perfect (fulfilled and completed) and show themselves most effective in [your] weakness. Therefore, I will all the more gladly glory in my weaknesses and infirmities, that the strength and power of Christ (the Messiah) may rest (yes, may pitch a tent over and dwell) upon me! 2Corintians 12:9 (AMPC)

God created us, loves us, and wants a relationship with us. If we only seek Him when we have trouble, then it's possible even though He is not the cause, He may let us see or experience some painful things as a means for us to call out for Him. He loves us unconditionally every single day and we should do the same. We should share whatever we're going through, by coming to Him everyday with our good news, sad news, hopes, and requests, because isn't that what a caring parent wants from their children? When children get older and start to make their own way in life, sometimes they get caught up in the fast paced and self absorbed world. Their attention is called in all directions, hardly leaving time to communicate anymore with their parents. Weeks, months, even years can fly by as they speed through their days. It seems like they only call their parents on holidays or when they're in some kind of trouble. In turn, the cycle repeats itself when those children are grown and their own children start becoming less dependant and more distant.

Of course I don't say that's true of all families, but these days we have all types of families that come with all types of challenges, so we need a good solid foundation if we want to build a loving supportive family.

Like any caring parent, your Heavenly Father loves you and misses you when you don't spend time with Him. If we try to live in the world without seeking God for guidance, first for ourselves and then for our children, we can expect unforeseen trouble, no matter how independent, resourceful and prepared we imagine ourselves to be in this life.

You can only be truly independent in this world by being fully dependant on the Lord. For in Christ, we become new creatures and heirs to all that is His, and we are no longer of this world which He has already conquered.

I have told you these things, so that in Me you may have [perfect] peace and confidence. In the world you have tribulation and trials and distress and frustration; but be of good cheer [take courage; be confident, certain, undaunted]! For I have overcome the world. [I have deprived it of power to harm you and have conquered it for you.] John 16:33 (AMPC)

Relying or leaning on the Lord was not so easy for me to do, even though it is the best thing that ever happened to me. It requires complete trust in God which I very much wanted to do and my heart knows I did try, but when I was tested, I struggled to believe, because I never experienced that kind of absolute trust with anyone ever in my life.

I don't mean I didn't trust people. I had a certain amount of trust with family and friends who have been there with me in bad or good times, loved me, cared about me, as I did them. However, I think we all have been let down by even our closest loved ones from time to time. That's because we are not yet perfect loving humans. We try to love unconditionally, we can forgive over and over, but it's hard to restore trust when it's broken, because love is not the same as trust.

In the beginning, God loved Adam and Eve, gave them a blessed life and trusted them to be obedient to His Word. Then they broke the trust by putting it in the words of the deceiver, who persuaded them to sin. Because of their disobedience we have deception and mistrust in the world, but God still loved them and still loves us. Trust has to be earned through a period of testing and since we are in a relationship with the Lord, trust is essential to grow our faith. We need to trust completely in His unconditional love for us or we will let fear hold us back from receiving His great promises for this lifetime.

The fear of man brings a snare, but whoever leans on, trusts in, and puts his confidence in the Lord is safe and set on high. Proverbs 29:25 (AMPC)

We do this by testing and proving the truth of His Word. He expects that we will do this and as we continually trust and follow Him, there will be times when He lets our faith be tested. This is mostly for us to realize our progression as He works in our lives to bring us to even higher levels of prosperity. We grow our faith by exercising it through obedience to His word.

So faith comes by hearing [what is told], and what is heard comes by the preaching [of the message that came from the lips] of Christ (the Messiah Himself) Romans 10:17 (AMPC)

We will see evidence of our activated faith by the good changes that happen in our lives along with answered prayers.

It had become a regular habit for me to spend time with the Lord and I believe His Word is Truth. As I mentioned earlier, putting my trust in God is something I wanted to do but found difficult in certain situations. To say I could have trusted someone with my very life was not something I could do before now. God not only gave me life, He gave me new life with a second chance when I became reborn, and still things that happened earlier in my life, made me hesitant to ask for help, a favor, or anything else.

During my life there were occasions when I had a great need and had to trust in someone for help, but I found that trust was broken or misplaced. Trust begins at birth with our parents and family, or at least it should, but I didn't have security in those relationships most of the time. So although I loved them, complete trust was never there for me. It carried over into my adult relationships with few exceptions and not having great expectations of trust greatly reduced my circle of friends. However God's love will always exceed our expectations. Through a period of testing, He brought change and blessings of healing, of love and joy and prosperity into my life and into the lives of my family, friends, and neighbors. He's not done working in me yet and He's given me hope filled expectation to accomplish good things! I feel like I'm just getting started and it all began with a measure of faith. With God, trust is a must!

I decided to test what I had learned so far. I heard one of my favorite preachers telling the Bible story of Jesus and the fig tree. Basically, Jesus saw a fig tree that already had its leaves, which meant there should be fruit under them. He looked but found no fruit, so He cursed the tree and then it died. (By the power of His Word) The preacher telling the story said, when he was younger he tested this out with a plant that was near his home. Whenever he would walk by it he cursed it in Jesus name, until one day he saw all the leaves turned brown. I knew this was something I needed to do, so I went to my Bible found the scripture. You can read part of it here for yourselves and I added a few more to affirm who we are in Christ.

And seeing in the distance a fig tree [covered] with leaves, He went to see if He could find any [fruit] on it []for in the fig tree the fruit appears at the same time as the leaves]. But when He came up to it, He found nothing but leaves, for the fig season had not yet come.

And He said to it, No one ever again shall eat fruit from you. And His disciples were listening [to what He said].

In the morning, when they were passing along, they noticed that the fig tree was withered [completely] away to its roots.

And Peter remembered and said to Him, Master, look! The fig tree which You doomed has withered away!

And Jesus, replying, said to them, Have faith in God [constantly].

Truly I tell you, whoever says to this mountain, Be lifted up and thrown into the sea! and does not doubt at all in his heart but believes that what he says will take place, it will be done for him.

For this reason I am telling you, whatever you ask for in prayer, believe (trust and be confident) that it is granted to you, and you will [get it].

And whenever you stand praying, if you have anything against anyone, forgive him and let it drop (leave it, let

it go), in order that your Father Who is in heaven may also forgive you your [own]
failings and shortcomings and let them drop. Mark 11:13-14, 20-25 (AMPC)

I assure you, most solemnly I tell you, if anyone steadfastly believes in Me, he will himself be able to do the things that I do; and he will do even greater things than these, because I go to the Father.   John 14:12 (AMPC)

For the word of a king is authority and power, and who can say to him, What are you doing? Ecclesiastes 8:4 (AMPC)

And formed us into a kingdom (a royal race), priests to His God and Father—to Him be the glory and the power and the majesty and the dominion throughout the ages and forever and ever. Amen (so be it). Revelation 1:6 (AMPC)

All around my house there are lots of fields and trees. Alongside the dirt driveway near the trees there was poison ivy growing. Whenever I went to get the mail at the driveway, I had to be careful, because I had several severe cases of poison ivy in the past and did not want to go through that painful itchy experience again. I couldn't use a chemical weed killer because there's a stream that runs by that feeds wildlife and farm animals. So after telling God my plan and pre-apologizing for killing His plants, I walked over to that poison ivy and said, "I curse you poison ivy in Jesus name!" I sounded a little weak in my delivery and I didn't think the plant would obey a wimpy sounding King (or Queen). I composed myself and with authority I yelled, "Be cursed poison ivy, in Jesus name you are condemned to death!" I was pretty sure the poison ivy heard me along with a few neighbors. That's OK, because they probably already thought I was a bit weird. I used to go outside and meow to get my wandering cat to come back home. With great reverence to my Lord and Savior, and all kidding aside, every day I went out to get the mail I spoke those words to the poison ivy for nearly two weeks. Then I went away for a while to visit someone.

When I got back I had forgotten about the poison ivy and went into the house to put my things away and then went to get my mail. I saw every poison ivy plant was covered in brown decayed spots! It almost took my breath away. I walked up and down the driveway and they were all dead.

There are two more things that made me know it could only be the power of God at work. All of the other plants and weeds were still growing untouched, while only the poison ivy was decaying in the midst of them. This was not some science experiment about yelling at plants because then all of the plants that were with the poison ivy should have died. Then one day soon after that event, my neighbor was across the road and I told him about my poison ivy and he said we didn't have any around here. I told him yes we did and showed him the same plants on his side of the road. He said "June, that's not poison ivy". "Huh?" I said, "Sure it is, I know what it looks like and I'm severely allergic to it!" He said, "No it isn't, it looks similar but poison ivy' is shinier". "Wow", I thought, "So what really happened here?" Well, I had faith in the name of Jesus and without wavering, believed it was indeed poison ivy and cursed to die. It happened because there is power in the words we speak as believers in Christ our Lord. Even in our daily lives, we should be mindful of what we speak about ourselves and to other people because our words have power to build up or tear down. The Lord told us we will eat the fruit of our words.

Death and life are in the power of the tongue, and they who indulge in it shall eat the fruit of it [for death or life]. Proverbs 18:21 (AMPC)

If we go around saying to anyone including ourselves, words like, stupid, loser, worthless, idiot, tired, ugly, depressed, failure, sick, trashy, etc… then we can expect to see negative results. Even if we are just casually saying something like, "I feel like crap, I have a pounding headache and my hair is a disaster Uhgg!" What kind of day can we expect to have? If we wake up and feel terrible, we can say something like, "Christ is in me and He is strong, healthy and looks fantastic so it's gonna be a great day! If we still need an aspirin, we can ask God to bless it to work quickly.

By the way, God will not assist us if we have wrong or harmful intentions toward someone. If we have a grudge against our neighbor because his dog poops on our nice lawn everyday, and we pray for the guy to break his leg, God will not aid bad intentions. However, we can pray for help to resolve the situation and wait for guidance form the Holy Spirit. We can also pray for patience while we wait. Our neighbor may not even realize we are upset or why. We can try buying our neighbor a pooper scooper and some dog treats and maybe the neighbor will thankfully take the hint.

The Lord is always with us working unseen and helping us even with little the things. One day I was taking a shower and when I opened the curtain to get out of the tub, there was a HUGE bee buzzing around the bathroom. If you have ever been stung by a bee you know *it hurts like*...well it hurts like a giant stinger stabbing you! I move really slowly getting in and out of the tub because of pain in my legs. I thought, "What am I going to do?" It's not like I had a fly swatter handy in there or even my towel which wasn't close enough to grab without encountering the bee. I said "Lord, please help me get out of here so I can somehow kill that bee".

I waited until it buzzed up near the ceiling and quick as I could, got out and shut the door behind me. I threw my robe on and went to get wasp killer which is something you keep in stock if you live in the mountains. I also got a fly swatter and headed back to the bathroom. Having no idea where the invader might be, I again prayed for the Lord to help me find and kill the massive bee which He created! Slowly I opened the door, listening for the buzzing and heard nothing but my own breathing. I looked around and listened and then saw the rug on the floor and there it was laying dead. I waited cautiously and held the swatter over it to see if it would move but no buzzing, no moving wings, nothing! It was dead, but I swatted anyway, scooped and flushed it. I have no idea how a bee got into the house because the doors were closed and the windows have screens, but I believe God did this for me to show He cares about even the smallest details of our lives. He wants us to lean on Him and trust in Him for the little things, the big things and every in-between thing.

He who is faithful in a very little [thing] is faithful also in much, and he who is dishonest and unjust in a very little [thing] is dishonest and unjust also in much.
Luke 16:10 (AMPC)

Since He already gave His only Son which is the greatest blessing, He would not deny us a lesser blessing, so increase your faith and trust in the Lord.

The next time I had something for the Lord to fix, I didn't hesitate long to ask for help. I wanted to help out at a community dinner which our church prepares a few times during the year. The problem for me was my legs, which are sometimes very swollen and painful to the point where I can't even bend them. At the time, just standing in general wasn't too bad but when I couldn't bend my right leg to get into the shower, I had a problem. I prayed to the Lord, if He wanted me to be able to help people, would He at least take this pain out of my knee?

It took about ten minutes of sincere effort to get into the tub and twice as long to get out after showering. Later when I went to bed I prayed a reminder to please help me. The next morning when I got up I had no pain at all. I was astonished that I could bend it with no swelling or pain. I thanked Him for His faithful well timed help, because for me, there was no other explanation needed. I was able to get through the community dinner and felt tired in a good way. Each time these things would happen my faith was increased and I was overjoyed to know I would always have the Lord in my life.

At the same time I was testing His Word, He was testing me. He tested me in small things and He tested me in some big things but He was always with me to lead me in the right direction.

[Born anew] into an inheritance which is beyond the reach of change and decay [imperishable], unsullied and unfading, reserved in heaven for you,

Who are being guarded (garrisoned) by God's power through [your] faith [till you fully inherit that final] salvation that is ready to be revealed [for you] in the last time.

[You should] be exceedingly glad on this account, though now for a little while you may be distressed by trials and suffer temptations,

So that [the genuineness] of your faith may be tested, [your faith] which is infinitely more precious than the perishable gold which is tested and purified by fire. [This proving of your faith is intended] to redound to [your] praise and glory and honor when Jesus Christ (the Messiah, the Anointed One) is revealed.

Without having seen Him, you love Him; though you do not [even] now see Him, you believe in Him and exult and thrill with inexpressible and glorious (triumphant, heavenly) joy.

1 Peter 1:4-8 (AMPC)

One summer I was visiting family and I went out to a nearby strip-mall for some groceries. It was a very hot day approaching one hundred degrees. I remember praying as I got in my car, to keep me safe and keep the car from overheating and to let me be a help to someone today. After getting my groceries, I got in the car and started to move out of the handicapped spot where I was parked. I saw an elderly lady with a small panting dog on a leash which she picked up as cars rolled past them. She was standing at the curb and looking around and seemed to me to be disoriented. I thought, "What the heck is this woman even doing out on a hot day like this?" I knew it was my opportunity to help, so I pulled my car nearer to her, rolled down the window and asked if she was lost. She told me no, but she was on her way to the dry cleaners and trying to remember how to get to that part of the mall. I knew there was a dry cleaner store near the end of the strip-mall, which was nearly a fifth of a mile away. I asked if I could please give her a ride there and then I would take her home if she would let me know where she lived.

I could not imagine having to walk all that way in this blistering heat, not to mention at her age or carrying the poor doggie. She agreed and thanked me as her dog hopped up on the seat and then barked for her to follow. The lady told me she lived in a senior center just a couple of blocks behind the mall. I asked her why she would come out on such an unbearably hot day just for dry cleaning. She said that was the day she always went and so she did. She was a very sweet soft spoken older lady and I offered a bottle of water for her and for her dog. The dog was happy to have it. I brought her to the dry cleaner, waited outside for her and then drove them to their home. We sat in the car and talked for a while before she had to go inside. She tried to pay me for the kindness but I told her not to worry, God takes good care of me. I found that I really enjoyed hearing her talk a little about her life and it made me happy, as simple as it was, that I could do something for her.

A good feeling remained with me all the way home. I thanked God for showing me, even though I still had healing to do, there are still opportunities to help others. I also prayed for more opportunities in the future. It's not that I never helped anyone before, because when I was younger and healthier and a situation called for it, I never minded helping. However, I didn't look to help on purpose and I guess like some people, I didn't mind helping out as long as it didn't interfere too much with my plans for the day. It was as if my brain told my eyes and ears to reject what it thought was too much for me to handle in my busy life. It was refreshing to know that God had given me a new perspective on what living life to the fullest means. I wanted to keep going and do good deeds until there were too many to count and to keep learning what He had in store for me next. There was a day when I got an example of how the Lord works all things together for the good of those who believe in Him.

We are assured and know that [God being a partner in their labor] all things work together and are [fitting into a plan] for good to and for those who love God and are called according to [His] design and purpose.
Romans 8:28 (AMPC)

Once again I was at a grocery store and while I was in line waiting to check out, I noticed the woman ahead of me ran over her budget and had to put some items back. She had young children with her and seemed to be having a hectic day. The children were sad faced when the mom put back their bags of Doritos. I felt that prompting tug on my heart from the Lord and I quickly grabbed the bags of chips and put them on my bill. I called to the mom and motioned her to come back. I quietly said, "God wanted your children to have these chips, so please take them". She looked a little shocked, but I smiled and said "please take them" and she smiled and said "thank you, really thank you".

The amazing part is, I wasn't trying to be noticed for what I was doing, and I usually shy away from attention, but someone besides the Lord saw what happened. A woman working there happened to be bagging groceries to help the lines move faster and she said, "God works in mysterious ways". She added, "This morning I prayed for two things, and one was to witness a simple act of kindness, and I just did." When we step out in faith to do something good, we shouldn't do it to be seen by others, but instead because it is part of who we are in Christ. Sometimes however, He gives us a little confirmation of how He works unseen and behind the scenes to bring us all together into His plan.

As I was learning to trust the lord more and more, I continued to test His word and He continued to test my obedience to His Word.

Ever since I contributed that first ten dollars to help, I had the desire to do more. Through each year I built up my contributions to certain outreach ministries until I was actually tithing, which means to give ten percent of our income. Since I had no more savings, I was living on my disability allowance from Social Security. I wondered how I was going to manage from month to month, but I set my mind to stick with God's plan. I had lots of medical bills, plus all the regular bills a person has, like shelter, food, water, taxes, heat, electricity, insurance, transportation, communication, etc… As it was, I juggled bills by paying less to some for one month and less to some others the next month, alternating back and forth. Things slowly began to happen as I put more trust in God and continued to tithe each month. God tells us to do what we can which is to give ungrudgingly to those in need, then He will be faithful to bless us by providing more than enough to share.

Bring all the tithes (the tenth) into the storehouse, so that there may be food in My house, and test Me now in this," says the Lord of hosts, "if I will not open for you the windows of heaven and pour out for you [so great] a blessing until there is no more room to receive it. Malachi 3:10 (AMP)

Things would go alright for a while as I started to catch up and then an unexpected expense would pop up. Things like frozen pipes and a toilet bowl that cracked, because I was away during a power outage that shut the heat off and it never restarted. Sometimes there were appliances breaking down or car repairs and more medical expenses. Yet somehow God fixed what I wasn't able to fix on my own.

The first few times of course I was worried about how I was going to deal with another expense. Physically I still had too many health issues to be able to hold a job for any length of time, but the Lord always found a way to send help. I hated, hated, hated to ask anyone for a loan. How timely could I pay it back if I did. I had done that in the past and it was not a good feeling.

Then when I was at my wits end, I would get a phone call or email from family or friends asking if I was able to do an odd job. Maybe I would house sit, look after a pet, proof read or edit some written material. I found the amount they offered to pay me was usually about equal to the amount of the expense I had. These were jobs I could do at my own pace, working around my disabilities, so I saw them as a blessing. The timing was perfect coming always when I had a sudden expense. On one such occasion, I knew that soon my car was going to need complete new brakes, but I also had a property tax bill which was coming due. Even though I tried to put money aside for the yearly taxes, sometimes I was behind and couldn't make the deadline, which only added a late fee on top of the bill. Just in time, one of those house sitting opportunities came along. I thanked the Lord and sighed in relief. It was a long drive to get there. I knew when I returned home I would like to get the brakes looked at because I could feel the jerky movement of the car as I applied them, which means they were wearing out.

A night or two before I was to leave for home; I was thinking how the Lord took my headache of these two expenses and turned it around, so I had almost enough money to pay for both of them. In the morning when I woke, I clearly heard the Lord say "**Pay your property taxes**". What an odd thing to hear. Of course I knew I had to pay them and I was already late, so I assured Him, "Yes Lord I will do that!" How wonderful to know the Lord cares about my finances. But the Lord knew me better than I knew myself.

After I was back home and settled in, it was time to refill my prescriptions and that meant driving to town 25 miles away and 25 miles back. I thought to myself, I really should get those brakes done before driving anywhere other than locally. I reasoned, if I paid the tax bill first, I would not have enough to get the brakes done for another two weeks. I really do need the car to be drivable in case of emergency. I then considered if I were to get the brakes done now, I would still be able to pay the tax bill in two weeks and be within the time frame before another fee was added. Knowing they would both be paid soon, to me the car seemed the more immediate need, so I made the appointment and took the car in to be fixed.

I prayed as usual before I left for the day, that Angels watch over and keep me and everyone else safe during the trip. The auto shop owner had also been the Chaplain for the local firehouse and while my car was being fixed we would sometimes talk about life in general or how God works things out in our lives. He was aware of how the odd jobs would coincide with my car repairs, coming just at the right time. When my brakes were finished being repaired I paid the bill happily and drove off to pick up my prescription refills.

A few miles before getting there, I was at a traffic light with no one behind me as turned to drive over a bridge that led to the road where the store was located. In the middle of the bridge I noticed a little old man maybe only five foot tall in a military uniform. He was walking slowly along in the right service lane. I thought, "Here is another opportunity to help, I'll see if I can offer him a ride". I checked the mirror, put my blinker on and slowly drove ahead of him into the service lane keeping my foot on the brakes when I stopped. I hit the button to roll down the window and asked if he needed a lift to the store or somewhere. He said yes and I unlocked the door for him to get in.

He opened the door and at that very moment I felt BANG! No not a gun, but a car had smashed full force hitting my rear driver side smashing it in and blowing out the tire. The old man spouted some curse words but was unhurt and he took off down the bridge road. I just sat there trying to understand what happened and see if I was hurt. My foot was still on the brake and the blinker was still blinking, so I put the car in park. So much for trying to do a good deed! How could someone hit a red car with brake lights and a blinking direction signal, in broad daylight that was stopped in the service lane? There was nobody behind me when I made the turn and it was several hundred yards from the turn to where I was stopped.

I seemed to be fine and I saw the person who struck my car had pulled into the service lane up ahead. I could see he was on his cell phone and I think maybe he was already on it when he hit me, otherwise I don't think he could miss seeing my car. I found out later he was an insurance agent!

Fortunately nobody was injured and witnesses who came over to check on me, had already called the police and also backed my version of the incident. Then I called my insurance agent, not to file a claim but to report what happened. As I waited for a tow to arrive, which by the way came from where I just had my brakes fixed, I realized that the Lord kept me and everyone else involved safe from harm.

Now I understood the importance of obedience to the Lord and to obey sooner rather that later. If I had paid my taxes as the Lord instructed, then I probably would not have been in an accident. Instead, I wasted my money fixing the brakes of a car which I could no longer use. Even though it was determined the other driver was at fault, it still required me to have lots of patience, waiting weeks for all the reports and claim paperwork to be legally completed, filed, processed and finally paid. I think they took their time, waiting to see if I was going to file a law suit, but I assured them I wasn't.

Meanwhile, I had no money to buy another car until they processed their claim, but they were not in a hurry. If you live in the hills, you can't get very far without a vehicle, or else you need to be in good enough shape to walk a few miles. I was not. Even that major car rental place, that claims *they deliver* a car to you, would not do so in my town. So I was very-very-very patient, knowing that God would work this out too. Eventually I got the check which was in my opinion a lot less than my car was worth, but I did not push the matter. I was able to find a similar car but it had double the mileage of my old car with a little extra rust. I was happy to have transportation again. Oh, and I did quickly pay my property taxes!

When I speak about the Lord testing my faith, being patient is part of it. Nearly two years to the date of that accident, I was hit again. I was near the NY-CT border in an older town that has very narrow winding roads. There's no shoulder along the roads to pull over until you get to the main street or closer to the highway.

I am not a hurried driver. I enjoy driving and I leave early and drive the appropriate speed for the road and conditions. I learned a valuable lesson as teenager when I was running for a bus and the driver saw me running but closed the door and took off when I was just three feet from the door. He just looked away as I stood there pissed off and out of breath, with all the people looking out the windows at me like they were glad it wasn't them. From that day on I never ran for a bus again. I learned to leave early enough not to be in a hurry no matter how I traveled.

So as I was driving on one of those winding 30 mph, roads, there was a man driving behind me and I could see how fast he caught up to me and I felt as if he was trying to make me go faster by staying as close to my bumper as possible. I was going the speed limit and I guess that wasn't fast enough for him. I couldn't even see his license plate because he was that close for at least a mile. I decided that I would pull into the service lane when I turned onto the main road and let this anxious driver go ahead of me. I stopped at the "T" intersection, signaled a left turn and then switched to my right blinker right after I turned, so he would know I was pulling over. I drove about three car lengths into the service lane and stopped. I waited and as turned to see if he was going to pass me yet, he slammed into my car. He only banged the back corner of my car but his was a lower car and he tore almost the whole passenger side off of his vehicle.

Once again I was sitting there wondering how is it that I am trying to do a good thing and now I suffer another accident. This person turned out to be a tennis instructor who was now late for his appointment. He got out of his car unharmed and waved his arms around yelled a lot about his car and eventually came over to me as I was still sitting in my car. He squawked, "Why did you stop? I didn't even see you; I was looking the other way for cars coming around the turn!" I wish I had my camera phone recording those words!

By the time the police showed up he had changed his story, saying I stopped short and he couldn't stop in time. However the policeman could see from where my car was and the damage to his car that he was not looking at the road ahead when he hit me. This time we traded all our information but I told the man I would not be seeking money for damages. I knew he was going to have to deal with enough of his own problems and my car was OK to drive.

I also had the chance to talk with him while we waited

and I mentioned it could have been worse than just car damage and maybe it was God's way of telling him to slow down. Maybe God kept him safe from something worse down the road. He wasn't offended and actually he thanked me for that. Maybe this was just the devil trying to aggravate me but it didn't work, because I knew God was with me and I was OK. I drove away and went about my day.

A few months later, after receiving three prior notices that they wanted to pay for my damages, I finally agreed to let the man's insurance person come and take a picture of my car. They cut me a check on the spot for a few hundred dollars. I'm sticking with God's way to handle things.

It's important to mention that these accidents were not caused by God. God is who protects us while events instigated by the devil or our own poor choices come against us. The Bible tells us that in this lifetime we all will have trials and tribulations while we're on this earth. Not one person can completely avoid times of trouble, but as believers in Christ we have the supreme advantage of His help and support to get through those times. If He allowed a situation to occur, then there is a reason for it even though we may never understand what purpose it served. I pray everyday, yet not once but twice someone smashed into my car. Even though I was initially shocked when it happened, I could feel His calming presence and it helped me to process what was going on and not react badly. Both times, the other drivers were visibly stressed and angry and tensions could have escalated if I reacted as they did. The Lord was teaching me to focus on and trust in Him and not my circumstances. Instead of getting angry over the damage, injuries, police, paperwork, repairs, and time lost, I thought, "Things could be worse, I am Ok and this too shall pass". We can't live full lives if we are expecting bad things to happen, in fact we should expect great things to happen, but if trouble does come we should know the Lord is always with us.

Another test came in the form of severe weather. I used to watch those weather chaser shows all the time when I was younger. I wondered what kind of crazy a person would have to be to drive into a storm looking for tornadoes. These are seriously dangerous weather events. They kill and destroy and leave rubble behind. Yet, I would sit glued to my TV in awe of the magnitude and power of them and the people who wanted to get as close as possible to the deadly elements. I wondered why people remained living in those areas and thought, "move away from there people!" Of course I understood that it's just not that simple to pick up and move your entire life or family on the chance that something might occur. For me, having poor health and losing my job became an opportunity to move up to the mountains, where I thought I would t least be safe from things like tornadoes.

One of the first summers after I moved there, a neighbor was having an outdoor party on his property across the road. It was late afternoon on a hot humid day and there was a live band playing 60's music. I could hear it from the deck of my house. The day started out sunny but then clouds rolled in, it got dark quickly and the rain began to pour. There was lightning and thunder, the likes of which I had never experienced before being up close and personal on the mountain. The booms of thunder made my house shake! The lightning was non-stop. I went from room to room watching the entire night sky light up in crazy colored bolts of pink and greenish blue with cloud to cloud lightning. The storm seemed to sit right over us and it looked as if I could stick my hand up and touch the clouds. I kept counting how long before each lightning strike and it was only 3-4 seconds and this went on for over an hour before there were any signs of the storm moving on. Finally it passed.

When I had a chance to speak with another neighbor I asked if that was typical of the weather up here. He told me there were only a couple of severe storms in late summer or sometimes spring, and of course, lots of snow. I said well "At least there are no tornadoes up here". He corrected me, "Oh yeah, we had a tornado here several years back. I squawked, "What, up here? ". He answered, Yeah, it came right through that part of your property and then across there" as he pointed to some mangled looking trees way behind my house. Well that was just not cool with me. I started looking online for details of past weather events and probabilities of another one. It could happen again. I also found through a friend in our environmental group, we had fault lines that ran through the area, which means we can have and did have earthquakes!

It was at that point I remembered I have to put my trust in the Lord, because He is my shield. There is no safe place other than under the wings of Almighty God in Heaven. We can build a bomb shelter underground and stock it with all kinds of supplies, but if we are elsewhere when the things we fear happen, then where is our escape or protection? We can't remain in that bomb shelter in constant fear and we can't take it with us wherever we go, but we can live boldly because of the promises of our God who is with us always. Even if we feel fear come over us, we need to remember that God is bigger and more powerful than anything that would harm us.

There was a time when a pretty big storm was on the way and it started out with just a steady rain. Everything was pretty muddy outside but after several hours the storm intensified. I received email alerts which said seek shelter in a basement or lowest floor because there was rotation with this storm. Rotation means a possibility of tornados. We have warning sirens in our town, but I can't always hear them where my house is situated or when diminished by other noise. I could feel the pressure in the atmosphere and I felt my blood pressure going up as I got a little panicky. Then the electric power went out and I was feeling the fear of not knowing what was coming. It was summertime and sweltering in my house with all the windows closed because of the storm. I went to the window to see if maybe I could open it a crack. What I saw was the sky had turned a blackish green with gusts of wind and hail pounding violently all over. I had a portable radio tuned to NOAH weather station that reported storm conditions headed in this direction may produce a tornado. My house was very small with no basement and at that point there was no where I could go. I took my Bible and my cat and went into a small closet and prayed. I knew the Lord was with me and I knew His word is true, and I knew I would be OK. With a flashlight I kept reading from Psalm 91 over and over until I stopped shaking and in about fifteen minutes the noise had died down and there was just a lighter rain falling.

He who dwells in the secret place of the Most High shall remain stable and fixed under the shadow of the Almighty [Whose power no foe can withstand].

I will say of the Lord, He is my Refuge and my Fortress, my God; on Him I lean and rely, and in Him I [confidently] trust!

[Then] He will cover you with His pinions, and under His wings shall you trust and find refuge; His truth and His faithfulness are a shield and a buckler.

You shall not be afraid of the terror of the night, nor of the arrow (the evil plots and slanders of the wicked) that flies by day,

Nor of the pestilence that stalks in darkness, nor of the destruction and sudden death that surprise and lay waste at noonday.

A thousand may fall at your side, and ten thousand at your right hand, but it shall not come near you. Psalm 91:1, 2, 4-7 (AMPC)

I went to the front door to look around and as I looked over the mountains I could see a long white spindly funnel to the South East which was in the next county. I realized I was living in the truth of God's protection. The tornado was later confirmed to have touched down in the next county.

There was even another time when we again had alerts for the same kind of severe weather and since I did not want to hear the booming peals of thunder that shook my house, I decided to wait it out at our church building which does have a basement. The radio reported the storm warning would stay in effect through most of the night, but a feeling had come over me that the worst part had passed. I went to the kitchen area of the church, checked outside the door and then closed it. It was still raining heavily. Then I Prayed, "Dear Lord, could you let me know when it's OK to go back to my house?" Within a few seconds time the red "**EXIT**" sign over the door blinked off and on again! I almost couldn't believe it but gathered my things and headed home laughing to myself and thanking God. In this life there will be times when we feel fear, and it's wise to take certain precautions according to each circumstance, but our first line of defense and protection is trustful prayer to the Lord. No matter where we might be, our Lord is there also and we need not fear. Amen!

There is no fear in love [dread does not exist], but full-grown (complete, perfect) love turns fear out of doors and expels every trace of terror! For fear brings with it the thought of punishment, and [so] he who is afraid has not reached the full maturity of love [is not yet grown into love's complete perfection]. 1 John 4:18

We live life free and bold when we let our faith in God take hold.

11- PARTING, PRUNING, PROMISES & THE PLATYPUS

To whom God was pleased to make known how great for the Gentiles are the riches of the glory of this mystery, which is Christ within and among you, the Hope of [realizing the] glory. Him we preach and proclaim, warning and admonishing everyone and instructing everyone in all wisdom (comprehensive insight into the ways and purposes of God), that we may present every person mature (full-grown, fully initiated, complete, and perfect) in Christ (the Anointed One). Colossians 1:27-28 (AMPC)

When a person becomes born again and the Holy Spirit takes up residence inside that person, there will be some home improvements taking place inside and outside.

Just like one of those home makeover shows, first we have to remove the junk, whatever is old, rotted, not working properly or of no use to us anymore. Then we can begin again with strong building materials that are up to code and will pass inspection. It's possible we didn't even realize our whole house needed rewiring or insulation. Once our foundation is solid and our structure sound, we try out some new colorful paints, add new furniture, appliances and personal accents to compliment our new decor.

Sometimes on those shows they use huge tarps over areas for protection to keep out the elements while they're working on the inside. From the outside there might not appear to be much going on, but inside there's a lot of prep work going on before things start to shape up. There's usually a big dumpster visible outside with all the waste materials tossed into it. So things might actually look worse for a while but it's all necessary if we want to get to the point where our beautiful new home is revealed. A home that is lovingly furnished, flowing with good energy and complete with a fully landscaped exterior. The grass mowed, weeds pulled, trees pruned, with a variety of flowers and fruit trees planted. And what a nice surprise, our house is now solar powered!

When I became born again, I had no idea that I was, or

even what that meant. I knew spiritual things were going on in and around me, but I used to think "born again" people were like the ones who shaved their heads and sold flowers at airports. When I heard an evangelical on TV referring to those who profess Christ to be their Lord and Savior as those who are born again, I was relieved I didn't need to shave my head or hang out at the airport.

Jesus answered him, I assure you, most solemnly I tell you, that unless a person is born again (anew, from above), he cannot ever see (know, be acquainted with, and experience) the kingdom of God.

Nicodemus said to Him, How can a man be born when he is old? Can he enter his mother's womb again and be born?

Jesus answered, I assure you, most solemnly I tell you, unless a man is born of water and [even] the Spirit, he cannot [ever] enter the kingdom of God.

What is born of [from] the flesh is flesh [of the physical is physical]; and what is born of the Spirit is spirit.

John 3:3-6 (AMPC)

The only requirement of being born again is to believe and keep on believing in Jesus Christ. Then it's important to remember that God loves us and already sees us as we are in Christ, so He sees us in our perfected state. He's not looking at our sins, our old baggage, or failures. He never stops loving us no matter how long it takes for us to realize we are being transformed into Christ.

The Holy Spirit in us even supervises the entire process so as we keep on believing in Christ, we can do what He has asked of us and that is to love God with our entire being and love others as we would ourselves. It seems almost too simple to those of us who are used to living in a fast paced over complicated world. We want answers to our prayers quickly, or to see evidence of our progression rate and we get fidgety when nothing seems to be happening. Then we even try to help things along by doing what God has not asked us to do, or at least not yet.

I remember when the Lord spoke to me and told me certain things would happen in my life and to be patient. I was super excited to know that and of course wanted to cooperate with His plan, even though I had no idea what that plan involved. I tried to continue doing good deeds whenever possible, but I didn't get out much because even with some improvements to my health I still struggled with daily pain, swelling and breathing problems. My heart was willing but my flesh was weak and I had to learn to live according to God's timing.

I found that if I wanted to get something accomplished, it had to be in slow and methodical increments with time to recuperate so I could keep going forward.

Even a grocery shopping trip could be an exhausting event. Some stores have motorized carts for the handicapped and that helps to get around, but not all stores have them. If I needed to walk through the store for my items, stand in line to check out, pack it up and then get it into the car, I was already in pain. Then I would need to return my shopping cart to the proper cart area. Putting the carts back seems like a ridiculously picky thing to do, right? I mean there are people who get paid to do that. I did it once in a while but never gave it a thought if I didn't return the cart. Then one day I heard Joyce Meyer, telling her own story about God asking her to put the cart back because it was the right thing to do. She explained how it took her a really long time to obey and I think it was two years until she could get it done every time. I'm a person who would rather skip the lesson and just take the test if possible, which means learning by someone else's example. Whenever I heard a testimony of God's way to handle an issue that I could relate to my own life, I tried to become obedient as quickly as possible and cross that thing off my to do list. I even prayed for the Holy Spirit to remind me if I was forgetting to do something, thinking it would be a great time saver. I'm not implying taking short cuts, because I have noticed with God, we're usually led to take the scenic route instead of the freeway, and it's always beneficial even when it's a longer route.

I never imagined I would have this relationship with the Lord and I began to see that for me there was no other way but to live in and with Him. I knew, if and when I was able to go back to work, that it would not be the sort of job I had before. It would be something that served God, which I believe was always part of His plan for me.

I could feel changes in my spirit and how as I kept reading the Word and confessing it out loud, I was better able to handle problems or changes, because I knew I was not alone. At first I thought, "I'm not sure I can do this or am I going to have to change all at once, and where exactly am I going?" But that's not at all how the Spirit works in our lives. We make progress a little at a time so we are not overwhelmed but enough that we are not discouraged.

As the Holy Spirit was clearing out debris and rewiring me inside, I tried to work on external things, by pruning my dead branches and tossing out things which were cluttering my life.

I had a large number of record albums, cassettes and compact discs which I collected over nearly 40 years, because music has always been very important and very present in my life. God did not ask me to do this but I thought I should willingly let go of this part of my past. I came to the realization, although I turned to music through my share of good times and bad times, when I became so gravely ill and in severe pain, I didn't want to hear any music at all. I had not played any music for many months even after I was saved.

It was a hard thing to do, I had music from every genre, but I knew a lot of it was not acceptable to God's ears. I gave some away and sold some and I backed up a select few onto my computer because some of the artists were telling their own faith journey through their music.

I found other things to part with like 40 pairs of old jeans and 100 T-shirts from concerts and other events. I took those and more clothes, coats, footwear and anything I wasn't using like small appliances, dinnerware, glassware, blankets, jewelry and packed them up. I donated them to our local thrift store or sold some at our tag sale to raise money for the church.

I didn't do all of that at the same time, but within a few years I did whatever helpful thing I could think of while I was growing my faith and waiting to hear each new thing from God. It felt good to be doing something and I was also making room in my house which was great because it's on the small side. It's surprising to see how much "stuff" we acquire over the years and what percentage of it we really use or need. The Holy Spirit helped me see how temporary our possessions are and to generously share what I have right now for another's need, while resting assured in the promise that the Lord will always provide for my needs.

Another branch that needed pruning was my TV viewing habits. I could definitely feel the work of the Holy Spirit with this one.

I have always liked to watch shows and action movies with cops and robbers, whether it was gunslingers or gang related. I loved suspense, thrillers, espionage, military drama, horror, firefighters, doctors, legal or courtroom drama, detective or scientific crime solving. If it had abbreviated letters or numbers in the title I probably watched it along with its spin-offs. I also loved comedy and nature shows and documentaries.

Basically I watched way too many shows and movies. During those first couple of years after being born again, whenever I turned on the TV, I felt like I was constantly channel flipping and losing interest. I didn't even realize why that was happening. I began to think, "What is happening to the writers of these shows or movies". They started out great, but then it seemed almost every show or movie was full of foul language, casual sex partying and gory crime scenes. For example, one show started out always focusing on the science and method of solving a crime after the crime had been committed. It seemed more recently to focus on the crime itself being committed and showing more bloody and grotesque detail with each episode. Who was changing, them or me, or was it a combination of the two? I believe it was a combination.

The more we as a society accept things as normal behavior, the more writers and producers will try to up their game and push the lines of what seems acceptable or normal. Not to mention the advertisers making prime time commercials that would have been X or R rated in the past! Have you noticed how some commercials take over the volume control on your TV's and electronic devices, even though you've *unchecked* that box?

There are some people in powerful positions, making tons of money from these shows and advertisements who want to continue by feeding us addictive junk food for our souls. They disguise it as awareness, being open minded toward our future and making progress as a society, which puts me in mind of a phrase I remember hearing a few times over the years.

Let us keep our minds open, by all means, as long as that means keeping our sense of perspective and seeking an understanding of the forces which mould the world. ***But don't keep your minds so open that your brains fall out!*** *There are still things in this world which are true and things which are false; acts which are right and acts which are wrong, even if there are statesmen who hide their designs under the cloak of high-sounding phrases.*

Walter Kotschnig November 8, 1939

Not only had I lost my appetite for destruction but also I curbed my enthusiasm for those types of shows or movies. As it happened, I was going to be away from home for an extended period of time and I canceled my satellite TV service, because I was unsure of my return date and didn't want to pay for something I wasn't going to use.

While I was away, I kept busy catching up on a lot of reading but I did watch a couple of favorite shows which included my daily doses of evangelical shows. When I finally did return home, I didn't immediately start up TV service, because I knew a few other people who didn't have TV service by choice, so I thought I would see how long I could go without signing up again. Soon enough, probably after a year, certain things happened that I could not have foreseen but God knew all along which made me happy and thankful to know I was headed in the right direction.

I received a large postcard in the mail advertising a completely new internet service provider now available in my area. I had been using dial-up for years and could not afford the crazy rates for wireless service from the leading providers. I did a little research and got answers to all the questions I needed to know before trying this service. The Lord knew my frustrations with dial-up service and I was patiently waiting for affordable high-speed service and here it was. Since I wasn't paying for TV service anymore, I could afford the new internet service. I even had a few bucks left over which covered the subscription cost for a network, where I could choose family friendly shows and movies to watch.

Not only that, but one day I was singing while doing the laundry and I wondered if I could find a decent radio station, knowing that up in the mountains there's mostly static. I found exactly three stations that came in clear. There was one pop, one country and one Christian. Not much of a choice I thought, but I left the Christian station on to keep me company. I couldn't believe what I was hearing. I remember the worship music I grew up with and the *limited selection* of modern Christian artists from the years I worked in the record store. What I was hearing now was new and upbeat and cool. The oddest thing about it was, for nearly every favorite band or artist I knew in the past, there seemed to be a Christian one with a similar sound. I don't mean a copy-cat version, but rather styles of music that I would have chosen to hear. The station is called 'The Sound of Life' and is listener supported, so they don't interrupt with commercials or sometimes even to let you know what artist is playing. At first I thought I was hearing new *CSN&Y*, *Eagles*, or even *Chris Cornell* from *Soundgarden*, but eventually found it was, *FFH*, *Dave Barnes*, and also the *Rhett Walker Band*. There is a *long* list of Christian artists out there making the best worship music I've ever heard, with some playing updated arrangements of traditional hymns giving them new life. If you want an example, look on the internet for an excellent tribute arrangement of

Creed, with *Third Day* and *Brandon Heath*. Artists like *Toby Mac* and *Mercy Me*, will have you on your feet and singing with joy and sometimes sharing tears with lyrics that hit your heart.

A number of these musicians have been around for decades while and others are brand new, and music genre lines don't exist. You don't know what you're missing until you've heard an electronic bluegrass artist and a rapper together on stage praising God. (*Crowder & Tadashii*)

Even just the title of *Crowder's* song ,*Run Devil Run*, makes me want to shout it from the hills! I could have filled the entire chapter with just the songs that resemble my own experiences on this journey. All of these artists were sharing their struggles with faith, lost and found testimonies of hope and gratitude in a most amazing way. Clearly the Lord has blessed them with their abilities to make incredible music, which is a gift for us all. After finding that one radio station I searched a little more and found there are many just like it across the country and online. In this age of technology we can share our worship, words and music wherever we go, because there is of course, an app for that.

I thought I was giving up music for God but He blessed me with a way to combine my love for Him with my love for music. Not because I did something good, but because He is always good and showed me a better way of living. I also found out about many outreach concerts and programs since that time and it was great news to know there's a bold new young generation with their own way to praise the Lord and bring hope to others. There are a number of Christian Churches across the U.S. and elsewhere who use this newer music alongside some traditional music during their services and they have thriving congregations. I got a sense that I would be sharing this powerful kind of worship music with a lot more people in the future. Meantime it seemed I was in need of more home maintenance.

We all have the same twenty-four hours each day and depending on what we hope to accomplish we divide our days into periods of sleep, eat, work, play, and worship. We do this all our lives no matter if we are in school, out in the workforce, or at home. Even though we should set a period just for worship during our day the Lord wants to be involved in *every* area of our lives. The best thing we can do for our busy schedule is to keep God in it. Some of us multitask and fill every minute of our day with attention divided in several directions and we're always on the go. We keep going, thinking we're invincible because that is the life the world is trying to sell to us. We say things like there's no rest for the weary, but there is rest when we cast our cares to the Lord.

Do not fret or have any anxiety about anything, but in every circumstance and in everything, by prayer and petition (definite requests), with thanksgiving, continue to make your wants known to God. Philippians 4:6 (AMPC)

The Lord is my Shepherd [to feed, guide, and shield me], I shall not lack.

He makes me lie down in [fresh, tender] green pastures; He leads me beside the still and restful waters.

He refreshes and restores my life (my self);

He leads me in the paths of righteousness [uprightness and right standing with Him—not for my earning it, but] for His name's sake. Psalm 23:1-3 (AMPC)

For me it was easy to devote time to the Lord, because I was almost always at home and trying to stay off my feet as much as possible. I did a lot of reading and listening to the Word, and I asked the Lord for clarification if I found something confusing. I was gaining spiritual and mental strength but still having challenges to my physical strength, yet I had a desire to be productive.

I could keep my legs elevated while I sat at my computer which was helpful. For a period of about four years, I spent many hours everyday doing research for our community environmental group which we formed around 2009. It became an intense political and sometimes legal battle. Since I wasn't physically able to attend many of the meetings or rallies, I contributed my time putting together material for our website or helping to organize meetings. I spent so much of my time staring at the computer screen, a blood vessel burst in my eye. It was gross to look at but not too painful. It was a hint that I needed to cut back a bit, but I found there was always more and more to do, and I was having a harder time getting things done or knowing when to quit for the day. Some members of our local group expressed they felt as if we were doing God's work and I agreed, it felt godly and it felt good, so I didn't want to give up helping.

At the beginning of it all I could feel the Lord leading me to find material that was relevant to this project. After a couple of years it became the focus of my day, consuming most of my time and energy. I began to notice I wasn't feeling very good physically and losing enthusiasm for the work I was doing and I kept running into unexplained problems with my computer and the website.

I also had conflicts about the way certain things were being handled, and I didn't feel the calming presence of the Lord with me anymore on that project. Toward the end of the forth year, we (all participants) had made a good deal of progress and we had a real victory in NY.

I posted a message to one of the involved listservs, which is like a group email used as a way to connect people from different areas to a common project. A post or reply can be sent to the whole listserv or to specific people involved in a conversation. In my post to the whole listserv, I mentioned giving thanks to God for helping us win this battle. Normally with this particular listserv there would be numerous reply posts from the group conversation, or at least 15 posted to me from individuals, especially when we were celebrating a victory. However, with this post in which I was sharing my joy there were zero replies posted to the group or to me, out of more than one thousand people. I was shocked at first and then I felt kind of sad. There were definitely some Christians in that group but I guess they were not comfortable mentioning God outside of the Church.

God doesn't live only on Sundays in a Church building. He lives in us wherever we are and we should not ever let others make us feel ashamed to share our faith. There was a letter written years ago by Thomas Jefferson to a Christian Church. It was about the, *Wall of separation between Church and State*, but its purpose was to keep the state government from interfering with Church business and not the other way around. It meant the government should not create any laws in reference to or regarding establishing a particular religious denomination in America, so we all remain free to exercise our faith of any denomination.

The U.S.A. was founded on biblical principles and when we lose sight of that we also lose our wisdom to thrive as a nation.

God created the earth and advised us to be good stewards of it, which is what I thought that listserv group was all about. I was sorry to find many of them didn't acknowledge our Creator or that *their abilities* to be good stewards also came from God. It was very soon after that when I had a message from God in a dream. Very simply on scrap of paper that looked like it was torn from the listserv email pages, were the handwritten words, "***remove me from this list***", written three times in a row. I knew that seeing it three times meant it was not just random or my imagination. I knew it was the right time for me to move on from the group and wait to hear from the Lord.

My point for mentioning the environmental group or state government was not to argue politics and religious freedom, but rather that whatever goes on in the world for better or worse, we serve a living God and have assurance the Holy Spirit will lead us whenever and wherever we need to go.

When we don't take time to pause throughout our day and check in with the Lord, we're missing a great opportunity to be refreshed and continue living in a balanced way. We can wind up overworked, stressed, eating and sleeping poorly, leaving no time relaxation and fun or even remembering how to have fun. Yes,

God wants us to have fun and laughter and joy in our lives. He created us with a sense of humor and also gave us things to laugh about. If you don't believe me take a look at the platypus. If you haven't seen one, try doing an image search online or at the library. The same God, who painted the graceful wings of a butterfly, also put together that wacky platypus. Seriously, what was He thinking, spare parts? He also told us to have childlike faith, because when we lose that quality, we tend to trust only in ourselves and our own capabilities to make our way in the world. When our time is overbooked we put serious, unnecessary strain and burden on ourselves and our families. Following Godly wisdom will keep our lives balanced so we can enjoy all the blessings He sends our way.

And said, Truly I say to you, unless you repent (change, turn about) and become like little children [trusting, lowly, loving, forgiving], you can never enter the kingdom of heaven [at all]. Matthew 18:3 (AMPC)

Except the Lord builds the house, they labor in vain who build it; except the Lord keeps the city, the watchman wakes but in vain. It is vain for you to rise up early, to take rest late, to eat the bread of [anxious] toil—for He gives [blessings] to His beloved in sleep.

Psalm 127:1-2 (AMPC)

O taste and see that the Lord [our God] is good! Blessed (happy, fortunate, to be envied) is the man who trusts and takes refuge in Him. The young lions lack food and suffer hunger, but they who seek (inquire of and require) the Lord [by right of their need and on the authority of His Word], none of them shall lack any beneficial thing. Psalm 34:8,10 (AMPC)

Delight yourself also in the Lord, and He will give you the desires and secret petitions of your heart.

Commit your way to the Lord [roll and repose each care of your load on Him]; trust (lean on, rely on, and be confident) also in Him and He will bring it to pass. Psalm 37:4-5 (AMPC)

When we find ourselves having endless days with no relief, we should ask the Lord to show us what things we need to change or rearrange and trust what He tells us. He already knows our desires and knows how to provide us with time for fun and laughter. I think that's why He created barbecue. I can almost smell it!

And Aaron's sons the priests shall lay the pieces, the head and the fat, in order on the wood on the fire on the altar.

But its entrails and its legs he shall wash with water. And the priest shall burn all of it on the altar for a burnt offering, an offering by fire, a
sweet and satisfying odor to the Lord.   Leviticus 1:8-9 (AMPC)

Even if all we can spare for fun right now is a minute, there's even clean comedy available online at Laugh All Night/Family Comedy Minute.

The Lord showed me something funny back when I still thought I was hearing from dead relatives. Maybe you've heard of the game where you combine pictures and letters to sound out a word puzzle. For example, a picture of a "box" + the letter "R" would mean "boxer". I had been in email contact with my cousin who I hadn't seen since I was a teenager. Not coincidently enough, he let me know that he also had a reawakening of sorts and he was following the Lord. Right about that time I had a clear vision in neon color which came in the form of a picture word puzzle. The message was, "C Q" along with a picture of "googlie eyes" like the kind in old cartoons when a car horn sounded "AOOHGA!" while the character's eyes would pop out. Then there was an "R" and a picture of the sun. Put it all together and we have, Seek You Our Son! So I thought under the circumstances this message must be from my Aunt and Uncle who had passed away, acknowledging that I was emailing their son who was my cousin.

Eventually I realized this like many dreams or visions I had, was coming from the Holy Spirit. These messages were to get my attention focused on seeking the Lord, but in such an amusing way. They must have had a BIG party up there when I finally caught on to all the messages. Not everyday with the Lord will be a party but every day will be better than any day without Him and that's a reason to celebrate.

One of those not so fun days came when I began to understand the Lord was leading me to end a relationship with a close friend who I had known for most of my life. This was of course my friend Simon Strange. It was four or five years since we reconnected and through that time we had become (in my opinion) better friends than we had ever been before. Even though he didn't live close by, we emailed regularly, spoke on the phone, worked on his book project and got together a few times during the year with friends.

It was an easy friendship to be in and we had fun most of the time but we could also confide in each other about more serious things if need be. Aside from being fun, interesting and knowledgeable, Simon was also a helpful person. When I explained that I had floor boards in my house that snapped through a bad winter, he offered to fix them, no charge because he's that kind of a person. He's gifted when it comes to arts or crafts and always willing to help a friend. He drove up with another friend, brought his tools, measured, cut, and hammered all day until all the boards were replaced.

While he had a lot of good qualities, he also had some that were not so helpful to someone who is just learning to hear from the Lord. Simon loved to "discuss" religion and politics in great detail. He could be persuasively persistent when arguing a point of view, which was not even necessarily his own, just to see if he could change a persons mind. He happens to be a one of those people who don't take things at face value if a subject interests him. He would dig and dig trying to find the cryptic value, sometimes even when it's the plain truth of the matter that matters. In politics it behooves a person to dig a little and do some research. (I love the word *behooves* because it sounds funny. I heard the actress Jami Gertz use it on a sitcom many moons ago and after all these years I finally found a place to use it.) Now in the case of religion, we of course should also be looking to find the truth. If we are not being spiritually satisfied by what we find, to the point of our lives being forever changed for the better, then we should persevere until we become satisfied in our spirit that we know the Truth. God's Truth is not hidden from those who seek Him. Jesus told us He is the Truth, the Life, and the only Way to the Father and what He speaks is of the Father.

We are also told to test and prove the Word because it

is the Truth and will stand the test of time. I know that we can hear all those things in church and still wonder if we are on the right track, which is why it is so important to read and study the Bible for ourselves. When we pursue knowledge of the Lord in faith, then He will find a way to reach us and we will hear His voice. There are other voices out there calling us in other directions but we can always know the voice of our Lord, because it will never go against His nature of holiness, goodness or what is revealed to us through reading the Bible. Once you know the Truth, nothing and nobody will be able to separate you from Him, and there will be no need to look elsewhere.

In the case of my friend Simon Strange and our discussions on religion, there came a point where I could feel a tug of war in my spirit. I was already hearing God's voice even before I knew it was Him and He was leading me where I needed to go, but I was a bit slow to understand or move.

As I mentioned earlier, the Lord had spoken to me regarding Simon and I even told Simon about it because I didn't realize what it meant. Then I had a second dream and a third dream regarding him, both of which I misinterpreted because I couldn't figure what I was doing wrong. The first dream took place outside by a tree, possibly where we saw the Mormon festival. We were sitting there having a conversation when all of a sudden I felt my attention drawn upward. From beyond the trees came a light filtered through the leaves and it began to move to a clearing as I kept following it. Then slowly dropping down from the sky was something that looked like the cab or coach part of an old horse and buggy ride. It was only big enough for one person and it was all black with white lace trimming. I looked up and saw a figure motioning his arm as is if to say come up higher, while I heard the words," **Death Cab for Cutie**". *Death Cab for Cutie* is the name of an alternative rock band and an even older song title, but within this dream I took the words and cab at face value and said, "Oh, is this the end, time to go?" "This isn't so bad, it doesn't hurt". As I started to put one foot into the cab, everything disappeared and I woke up. At the time I didn't know what to make of the dream except that if I was going to die soon at least it wouldn't hurt.

I didn't mention the dream to Simon and just kept our relationship as it had been. We were emailing back and forth pretty much on a daily basis, not always about religion but the subject came up often enough. An odd thing began happening whenever I saw an email from Strange. I looked at his name on the screen and immediately someone else's name from my past popped into my head. It happened so many times that I thought I was going a little bit nuts. It even started happening when I thought about calling him on the phone. *Boom!*, another name was in my head. I had no explanation for this, but after some months went by I had another dream. This time I knew I was at some sort of school and the phone on the teacher's desk rang and the teacher said, "***It's for you***". I was handed a written message that read "***Work with us not against us***". I really did not understand that both dreams were about my relationship with Simon. I reasoned that maybe the death cab was symbolic for leaving something behind and moving on and that by the written message, I hadn't done it yet. I prayed about it because I surely didn't want to be working against something God wanted me to do. I looked around my house and thought about where I came from, where I was now and where I was going. All I could come up with was maybe I am not completely letting go of the past because I had reminders everywhere. I actually started throwing out some pictures of friends and acquaintances from my past. In the middle of that I thought, "This can't be right". These were just pictures in a box and I hadn't even looked at some of these for years so I said, "Help me Lord; I don't know what to do".

It was soon after that I had a clear vision that I needed to end my current relationship with Simon Strange. In this vision, I was somewhere talking with Simon and then my vision was blocked by a hand that was so close to my face, I could see the tiny reddish-blonde hairs growing from the skin, which appeared to be sun-burnt and surely matched the Teacher in the mirror of my other vision. It never occurred to me that Simon was actually distracting me from making progress in my relationship with the Lord. If He sent this person into my life, why would I think it's time to say goodbye, and would it be forever? Now I understood that the black cab was there to symbolize the death of my old relationship with Simon, while the white lace was symbolic of the Bride or the Church, which is my new relationship in Christ. The written message meant I was working against the Holy Trinity's plan for my life to prosper and grow. The more time I spent with Simon, debating theory or philosophy of religion from countless points of view, the less time I had to spend with the actual Teacher, and the true source of all I needed to know.

This was one of the hardest things I had to do so far in my life, yet I knew the Lord would help me take steps to get it done. I also knew I couldn't do this quickly like ripping a bandage off a wound, over and done and stings for a minute. Simon Strange was someone I'd known for most of my life, someone I liked, grew to love and care about. What helped me most was now the message the Lord spoke to me years earlier about Simon, had greater meaning than I first realized. It also meant that Simon was saved and he too was loved by God.

The Lord used my relationship with him to get me to a place where I needed to make my choice. He was asking me to heed the calling on my life by either choosing what the world offers or choosing the life He planned for me. Like I did as a little child, I chose God. The Lord never told me anything bad about Simon only that I was being distracted. It was true, and from then on I could feel uneasiness in my spirit with each conversation I had with Simon. Even though I was slowly tuning away from him, he seemed to understand why and he never became angry with me and I sincerely hope I was not the cause of any hurt to him. While I worked on putting distance between us, I also prayed that God would watch over him and if He saw fit, let me know if someday we might be friends again. Even though it was an easy choice to make, there was sadness in saying goodbye to my friend which was not easy.

And Peter said, See, we have left our own [things— home, family, and business] and have followed You.

And He said to them, I say to you truly, there is no one who has left house or wife or brothers or parents or children for the sake of the kingdom of God

Who will not receive in return many times more in this world and, in the coming age, eternal life.   Luke 18:29-30 (AMPC)

12- THE LORD'S POETREE IN MOTION...

The people said to Joshua, The Lord our God we will serve; His voice we will obey. Joshua 24:24 (AMPC)

With newfound time on my hands, I wondered what my hands should be doing with all that time. I definitely spent plenty of it reading my Bible, devotionals, other related books and still had time for watching my favorite preacher-teachers online. But to have a balanced life, we have to take what we've learned and apply it to a variety of daily activities. I knew I could be doing other things so I prayed for direction. As Christians, there comes a point where we need to step out in faith if we want to live the kind life only the Lord can make possible. I was pretty sure I was doing whatever the Lord asked me to do, but He wasn't speaking to me every single minute, day, week or even every month.

Even so, as I mentioned before, the Bible is a great reference manual. Throughout those pages we see Jesus as our living example of walking in love. Not all of us were meant to drop what we're doing and head out on the same type of lifelong mission as Mother Teresa did, but we are all called to do something in our lives. Our mission can simply be to glorify the Lord's name by graciously receiving His gifts, using them to prosper and share our blessings with others. That is how we can praise the Lord. If you have a God given gift in a particular area, you can find a way to share it. If you are a great mechanic, maybe the Lord will enable you to open your own service shop as you gratefully fix some vehicles for free, to those who are less fortunate. Maybe you're a mom or dad with seven kids and the experience you've gained through raising them, will be a valuable gift to share with new parents. If you work in a busy office and know how to keep organized, maybe you can also organize a fundraiser for a worthy cause.

My point is, that we are not all called to do the same thing and I'm not in any way suggesting that someone should do all the things I am describing in this book. In my heart I believe I was always meant to work for the Lord, and even though I screwed up countless times in my life, He still loves me and led me to share my story. All I had to do was ask and He led me step by step. Just as I love writing, He will take what you love to do and make it work to bring good things into your life. Some of us don't know what true happiness feels like until we learn to trust in the Lord.

Because of my disabilities, I wound up with lots of time as a captive audience but was willing to learn. We need to have a good attitude, which includes being patient, humble, forgiving and willing to make mistakes as we go forward. If we let pride become an obstacle, find fault and blame others, we won't get very far or accomplish very much in God's plan for our lives. I've experienced bumps and bruises from stepping out in faith and learned a bunch of things I was never meant to be. But I also learned, before I could do what I was meant to do, I needed more preparation. God's plan for us isn't always what, where or when we think it should be, so we make *little* plans of our own. I highlight little plans, because God's plan is always perfect, bigger and better than anything we could imagine. Sometimes we try to do something or get somewhere ahead of God, only to look around and find out we left Him behind. Fortunately we are permanently and lovingly tethered to God, so like toddlers, we can't' ever get too far from His help.

I won't go through *all* my recent failures but here are just a quick few from my born again years.

I love animals. When I first moved to this small town, I noticed there were lots of farm animals, wild animals, and especially near my house there were feral cats. I was more of a dog person and there always seemed to be one in our family, but I didn't mind cats. A big grey cat used to leap up and sit on my front deck all day as if he belonged, so I just let him stay there. Eventually I named him Charley and I sometimes fed him leftover food.

One day Charley brought over his pregnant wife. I had no idea he was out at night trying to get married. Soon Charley had a wife and two kittens. They lived under my deck for a while but his wife took the kittens and left town. Or maybe they just went as far as my neighbor's barn. Almost everyone in the area has a barn and barn cats. There always seemed to be cats rambling from one property to the next chasing field mice and finding a comfortable place to sleep. I found out from a neighbor, there was a woman who lived down the road who had dozens of cats outside, but she passed away so they just roamed the fields.

As it turned out, one Spring I took in a white and black kitten who wandered into my house when the door was open, as her sibling stayed outside. She had the nerve to walk in, climb up on my couch and inch her way over to sniff at me as I sat and watched. When I moved, she ran away but she came back in again. This time I waited till she was closer and I grabbed her and started to pet her. She immediately purred and very loudly. That was it, she was mine. I would have loved to have a dog, but I wasn't able to physically take care of one because my property wasn't fenced in and I wasn't able to walk a dog on a leash. I was allergic to the kitten (but you know how cute they are!) so I kept a supply of asthma inhalers and wet-wipes handy and we got along just fine. When she meows it sounds like she's calling Alice, Alice. I named her Trixie, after Norton's wife who always called out for Alice on The Honeymooner's show. The other kitten was brown and lived outside. It would come by to say hello now and then but did not want to be an indoor cat.

I fed four or five outdoor cats during the winters. I called around but there was no room in any nearby shelters and I didn't have funds to pay for getting them all neutered or even the ability to catch them, so that's the way it stayed for some time. One time I was away for a week or so and I returned expecting to see the brown cat come by for a visit but it never showed up. Concerned for nearly a week, I prayed to the Lord, if He would show me the brown cat was OK, then I would take care of him and all the other cats as well. Hmmm. Remember when I mentioned that as Christians the words we speak have power, or the Lord hears all of our prayers, or the Lord tests us? This is why I mentioned that.

The next day, the brown cat showed up with friends. There were at least a dozen cats that I had not seen before plus a few I remembered. They were all around the property and meowing. I thought, "God did you do this?" Then I heard, "**You did this when you prayed**". That time I wasn't sure if it was my own voice or God speaking to me, but I knew it was true. We should carefully consider what we are really asking for when we pray. Now I felt the obligation to feed these cats too, so I did. This went on for quite a while until I discovered other people were dropping off their unwanted kittens on my property. This was a huge problem to deal with. I was spending money I didn't have on bags of food and even medical supplies because cats get into territorial battles and get injuries. I couldn't walk outside without cat's following me. They weren't aggressive, but I could barely breathe outside my own house and walked around hooked to an oxygen machine. Everywhere I turned for help was a dead end and believe me I did try many options. Then eventually I remembered that the Lord is on my side and He forgives and helps when we call on Him in our troubles. Once again I prayed for help to care for and find homes for these cats, which by that time multiplied to around twenty. It did *not* happen quickly or easily and there were tears involved, but eventually they were all gone, and so were the cats.

I decided for the time being, I would just keep my one cat who by the way, liked to get out and go exploring once in a while, so I also had to find homes for her four adorable kittens. Shortly afterward I got her spayed. Then there was the time she brought home a snake and meowed loudly until I came to see her new toy. I picked it up and tossed it back outside. She zoomed out and brought it back inside. It's possible she thought she was a dog and we were playing fetch. So that was her last trip outside without a leash. From all of this I learned I was not cut out to be a cat farmer and my adventures in critter sitting would be limited to domesticated indoor critters in *very small* batches. Sigh!

I mentioned earlier there was a week I was away from all the cat issues and I was visiting my sister. The night before I was leaving for home, we had dinner, stayed up talking for a while and then I went off to the guest room, watched some TV, read a few Bible chapters and went to sleep. The next morning I woke and the Lord spoke to me and said, "***You will do this for a period of one year***". I'm not sure if there was more to it or not. By the time I realized I was hearing His voice, I was already moving around or yawning and I thought I heard something else but it faded. What was I supposed to do for a period of one year? I quickly apologized asking, if I didn't hear correctly, would He please tell me again? I waited a while but nothing happened.

When I got home I prayed again, letting God know I really wanted to obey but I didn't know what I was supposed to be doing. What if He never told me again? I had kind of a "Yikes" moment. However, on the third morning He spoke to me saying, "***Continue reading your Bible and you will know your purpose***". He also said something which I will keep to myself, but it was good and good to know because of what came next.

It had to do with a sermon I was watching on how God lets us step out in faith and stumble sometimes, so we can learn how to get up and keep going. I kept noticing that from time to time I was experiencing the very things I was reading in the Bible or hearing in sermons. It was a really exciting thing to see for myself how God was working in my life and in the lives of my family. I was putting two and two together and said to the Lord, "Oh…, OK Lord; I see what you're trying to get me to do. Good for you Lord, because I need that". To which the Lord said, "**Do Not Patronize Me, I Will Not Abide**". Wow! The feeling that I had disappointed the Lord with such a foolish thing to say was enough to make my heart sink. I just sat there sickened and told Him how sorry I was, knowing He forgave me already but feeling guilty just the same. It's not a feeling I ever wanted to experience again, but of course if I dwelled on it, I would probably find a reason I disappointed Him on a daily basis. Instead I dwelled on the good thing He said to me just a couple of days earlier. In this life we are going to make mistakes but when you know God loves you no matter what, it makes it that much easier to apologize and keep moving.

After I moved on from my cat fiasco, I also found I wasn't called to be a gardener. I tried growing fruits and vegetables in big raised beds or flower pots because my property seemed to be eighty percent rocks. I thought I could share my "bountiful crops" with friends and neighbors. My tomatoes were still green in October. My strawberries got eaten by the wild life. My morning glories never woke up and my blueberry bushes never bloomed. The only thing that actually grew was a pumpkin under my deck, and that was because my Halloween pumpkin froze, fell from the deck, decayed and found its way into some soil all by itself. At least I had a new pumpkin for next Halloween. Just a little example of how God works when we stop struggling to make something happen.

Finally I had a vision with a sign of what I might try. This was a vision of an actual green and white street sign in our town called "Cook" Street. It had arrows at both ends. I wasn't sure if it meant to cook food, or join the library which was the only thing in the direction that one arrow pointed. The other direction was toward the cemetery and oddly enough sort of a dead end. I do love to cook and had already become involved with the church community dinners, so I continued but wasn't sure it had anything to do with the street sign. Our church was very small and we had only around eight people who prepared and served the dinners, but together we always managed to provide 40-60 meals for the community. We were all pretty exhausted afterwards but, to see people in our community sitting together laughing and enjoying the food we prepared was well worth the effort.

Then I had an idea and the elders in the church gave me the OK to do a summer free lunch program for school kids in the area. I worked the budget out on paper, to show what our cost would be per meal and how many we could provide each day, with lunch-packs for over the weekend. I made phone calls, sent emails, went to talk with the proper people in the school, found financial support from the community and also volunteers for supervision and serving. It should have worked out great. But somewhere in dealing with the school, while at first they seemed very interested and helpful, my plan was never officially approved. I wasn't even given a reason. When I tried to follow up by speaking with someone on the phone or in person, my attempts were met with awkward words like, "I'm not quite sure where we are with that', or "I'll relay the message for you". Maybe they thought we weren't providing enough for every single kid, so let's not even try. Maybe being a public school, they put politics before welcoming help for the kids from a community church.

It's not that I was giving up on a project because of a little difficulty. It's more like learning to have a godly sense of direction by which doors were closed in my face. In the past I might have become confrontational in this situation, but I had to accept this project wasn't going to happen, put it in the past, forgive and move on to something else. It was not the Lord's plan for me to begin this project, so even though I was trying to do something good, I didn't feel the presence of His peace to pursue the matter.

Next, a friend told me of an opportunity to join a group

that helps fund our free library which is on Main Street at the corner of "Cook" street. I wondered if maybe this was why I had the vision of the Cook Street sign. It was started by a handful of wonderful women volunteers who wanted to raise funds, for new library programs and to renovate a building for expansion of the library. These women were all very creative and put together luncheons, auctions and sales with lots of enthusiasm, dividing the tasks according to people's talents and abilities. At least I was talented enough to stuff lots of envelopes. Well actually, I did have a blast organizing one of the cookie sales and we beat the sales total from the previous year, so that was good. It was something I could do without being on my feet too long and I made my own time schedule so I could rest when I needed it.

After that I was asked to fill a vacant spot for the library Battle of the Books, which was a reading contest between neighboring schools. All I had to do was sit there, use a stop-watch and signal the kids when to answer a question. I got there early and helped set up a few chairs and tables and then the battle was ready to start. In the middle of the very first round, I felt overheated and lightheaded. I barely finished the round and had to stop. I think it was not a coincidence just as that was happening, a teacher not scheduled to be there walked into the classroom and was happy to sit in for me. Although I liked working with this group of volunteers, I didn't feel that this was exactly what I was supposed to be doing and after about a year I bowed out. Even a used bookstore which the library opened on Saturdays might have been a fun place to help out, but it was down lots of steps in a musty basement, which is exactly what I need to avoid.

Mentally, wanting to help was easy but physically, being able to help was tricky. Taking several medications at the same time made simple things overcomplicated. I would feel fine one minute and a slight change in temperature could make me dizzy or short of breath. Too much time on my feet and there's pain and swelling to deal with in my legs. It was kind of frustrating to feel like I was supposed to be doing something but failing at everything I tried, because I didn't know what that something was yet. Eventually I came to realize there was a group home for the handicapped located on Cook Street, and I considered all my aches and pains would actually be a benefit in understanding how to work with people effectively in that environment. I fully expected that I would be healed in God's timing and in the meantime, I was still happy to know I was making progress a little at a time.

When I'm happy I want to share my happiness with others. I'm not sure if everyone becomes this way when they first understand they are hearing God's voice, but I was beyond excited and a tiny bit over zealous. It was like winning the lottery and telling friends, family and neighbors that I wanted to share the winnings with them, but they thought I was joking. Some of them said that's nice for you, but we don't necessarily need your money because we have some of our own. Some looked at me like I was crazy, but they kept smiling for as long as I rambled on about my winning ticket. Some let me know that they would like to believe I won the lottery but they had not seen any proof that I had the winning ticket or physical evidence of my winnings. That's when I began to realize, on the outside I looked pretty much like the same person I had always been. People closest to me could tell that I was happier and my health had slightly improved but the seeds of faith planted in me were just beginning to sprout, so I wasn't visibly bearing any fruit yet. I had changed so much spiritually and mentally but I understood there was more to do before some people would believe the good news I had to share.

Then the Lord put big dreams in my heart by asking me, "**What do you want in life**". I told Him, "I don't want people to hurt". From just that one question and answer, came a burst of confidence and ideas of how I was going to be able to reach out and help hurting people. It was like visualizing a pinpoint on a map and then seeing lines traveling out from it in many directions but all connected to each other and to the original point. There were times earlier in my life when I pondered the very things I was now dreaming about, but I lived my life with no real hope in my heart that I could do them, short of winning the lottery. Hearing the voice of God, means Jesus already paid for the only ticket I would ever need. God not only has a plan for our lives, He supplies us according to *His* riches with whatever we need to accomplish that plan, when we rely completely on Him.

I began to write some of the ideas on paper and do a little research on how to go about setting up non-profit organizations or foundations. Right away I could see I would need to raise money before I could raise more money. Since I had no money and was still not physically able to work, I wondered how God was going to get me from point A to point B.

I decided He might need me to help Him out with that one, so I tried buying a few lottery tickets. If I won a dollar or two I reinvested in more tickets. I think once I won $25, so I thought God was OK with this lottery idea. I even tried that other thing by mail, where they let you know *you may already be a big winner*, but I wasn't. Then I saw a video of a woman who actually won the big bucks and she thanked God. I figured since I was going to do good things with the money, surely The Lord would hook me up too! I asked the Lord to please bless my lottery ticket. I brought the ticket home and put it next to my computer so I would remember to check the next morning if I had won. When I didn't win I was a little sad and then I clearly heard, "***I will not encourage gambling***". Uh-Oh, chastised again! Why does my wisdom come only after I do the crazy thing? What would make me think the Lord needs my help to do anything? Obviously the Lord was taking me along the scenic route to prosperity, but I tried to follow a detour sign with a lump-sum-payment option.

I wondered what I could do in my current physical condition to raise the funds I would need to start my project. It had to be something I could do from home while on medications or machines and without a specific time schedule. I looked into those work at home jobs for people with disabilities and found it to be busy work on the computer or phones, which was fine. However the rate of pay they offered me was very low. They claimed that was compensation for not having train or bus fare and I did not have to drive to work, so no travel and mileage or gas expense. I disagreed. Sometimes I used to walk to work, so now what? In addition, they required me to upgrade my current data plan and I was expected to pay for this even though I was using it for their needs. It felt forced, unfair and didn't seem to be a good move at that time.

As usual I prayed about the situation and asked if this was the way the Lord wanted me to proceed. I don't mind working; I had done it all my life. Now I had bigger dreams, so if and when I was able to work, I needed a job with more of a purpose than just to have one. I was delighted to find that after I prayed about it, lyrics from an old song titled "Free Your Mind" came to me courtesy of the Holy Spirit. The song tells about how *freeing your mind* from wrong thinking will *open it to the rest* that is to come. It made me realize I was again trying to make something happen by over thinking and trying to adapt God's plan into my own. I know I can do all things in Christ who gives me strength, (Philippians 4:13) but that doesn't necessarily mean I should do *all* things. We are in Christ as partners, so we should do our part and He will do His part. The challenge for me was figuring out my part and letting God be God in my life. The songs theme also had a double meaning of *rest* in this case. The Lord tells us many times to *fear not* or *worry not* about things, (free your mind) and if we trust in Him we can find *rest* from our concerns. He already knows what we need, and when we stop trying to figure things out and lean on Him, everything else (the *rest* of it) will follow, falling neatly in place.

And which of you by being overly anxious and troubled with cares can add a cubit to his stature or a moment [unit] of time to his age [the length of his life]? If then you are not able to do such a little thing as that, why are you anxious and troubled with cares about the rest? Consider the lilies, how they grow. They neither [wearily] toil nor spin nor weave; yet I tell you, even Solomon in all his glory (his splendor and magnificence) was not arrayed like one of these.

But if God so clothes the grass in the field, which is alive today, and tomorrow is thrown into the furnace, how much more will He clothe you, O you [people] of little faith?

And you, do not seek [by meditating and reasoning to

inquire into] what you are to eat and what you are to drink; nor be of anxious (troubled) mind [unsettled, excited, worried, and in suspense];

For all the pagan world is [greedily] seeking these things, and your Father knows that you need them.

Only aim at and strive for and seek His kingdom, and all these things shall be supplied to you also.

Do not be seized with alarm and struck with fear, little flock, for it is your Father's good pleasure to give you the kingdom!

Luke 12:25-32 (AMPC)

As I thought about that tune, it put me in mind of the music I used to listen to in my early twenties and also a particular incident that happened on a camping trip. One summer I went wilderness camping in the Adirondacks with some friends. Wilderness camping just means there are no actual rentable campsites with utilities for convenience. You park and walk way into the forest, bringing *everything* you need or you do without. After we set up camp, we did quite a bit of wandering around and by the time night came we were giddy from being exhausted. We were also drinking and some did more than that, but not me. We were joking around, having fun being a little crazy outside with nature and enjoying the campfire.

Surrounded by all the gorgeous trees in the forest, I decided to make up a silly campfire story about trees and the idea of recycling. I have always loved trees and used to ponder the process of how a tree becomes a page of paper, sometimes referred to as a leaf, as in loose leaf for a binder. Basically, as we were sitting around the fire laughing and drinking, I stood up, hushed everyone and began to dramatize my tall tale of how, *the trees listen to us and can absorb our words through the air, or even by the roots through minerals of decayed bodies. Then they form our words into story-buds and become written in the leaves. Some people have the ability to tell the stories by eating or reading the leaves*. OK, let's not forget we were tired and tipsy, and it sounded funnier at the time. To me the weirder part was, my friends all thought I believed my story was the truth, because I might have been under the influence of a hallucinogenic drug. I was not! They tried to get me to sit down, take it easy and everything would be fine. I could not convince them I made it up and I was not tripping! The next morning they were talking about my behavior asking if I remembered any of it. Of course I did, and I repeated it to them. Good golly Miss Molly, were my friends that gullible? If I had been under the influence, chances were I wouldn't remember the details, but I'm remembering the truth even as I type it now.

The tree story kept popping into my mind over the years so eventually I jotted it down wondering if it had a purpose. A couple of decades later, I thought of a way my friend Simon Strange might be able to use it in connection with his short stories, but there was something personal about it and I kept it for myself. Possibly because once while I was looking up something to do with my family history, I was surprised to find that my last name of Abele, actually means, *white poplar tree*. So when I found myself remembering my tree story once again, an idea came to me and all of a sudden I was writing a poem to the Lord, about a tree. It was describing my spiritual journey and rebirth in the Lord. I called it, "Sing a New Psalm..."and this particular tree was called "The Lord's Poetree". (See end pages)

I realized I had several of these kinds of poems and I began working on putting together a website. This was a way to praise the Lord and invite others to share their poems, art, photographs, etc... from there I could offer T-shirts and other merchandise to raise funds for a non-profit organization. I collected my poems, roughly sketched out my tree concept for the website which became TheLord'sPoetree (.com). It felt as if all of this had been dormant inside me, just waiting to come alive. While putting "TheLord'sPoetree" in motion, I found there are a lot pieces and expense to building a website, even with the do-it-yourself kind. This included buying the domain, the site, the trademark, the mailbox, formatting and designing it all to be user friendly. It was a time consuming project but I knew it had potential to expand and include music, or even an interactive treemap locating where branches and leaves were growing, with translations.

It was exciting to finally be able to do something creative for the Lord Who saved me. I was so full of love and joy that I bought the domain (website name) on Valentine's Day and launched the site on Father's Day. I'm just so cute and clever, ain't I? Well maybe not, because if you look for the site as of today, you might not find it, but please look for it in the future. I *temporarily* disconnected the domain until I could devote more time, resources, and add professional upgrade. Meet me in the next chapter and I'll tell you why that happened.

13- NO COINCIDENCES & NO DEGREES OF SEPARATION

Who shall ever separate us from Christ's love? Shall suffering and affliction and tribulation? Or calamity and distress? Or persecution or hunger or destitution or peril or sword? Yet amid all these things we are more than conquerors and gain a surpassing victory through Him Who loved us. Romans 8:35,37(AMPC)

24/7- that is how God watches us. He is ever present with us. When you really start to understand what the means, you begin to see signs of His presence everywhere you go and you will find just how enjoyable your life can be if you follow where He leads.

Shortly after I began working on organizing my poems for the website, I had the opportunity to use my sister's swimming pool while she was away from home. Exercising was very difficult for me because of chronic pain and swelling in my body, along with a chronic lung disorder. However, I could exercise all day in the water with no pain at all. Swimming increased my blood circulation and helped my breathing tremendously. For six weeks I was able to build muscle, lose weight and I was feeling much stronger. My mind and body were relaxed and I could sleep well at night. A few days before I was to return home, I picked up some kind of virus or flu, which left me in worse shape than when I first arrived there. I was shaking all over with chills and then fever and I had a headache so severe, I thought I would need to call for an ambulance. I never experienced head pain like that before or since that time. After shaking continuously for three days I found I wasn't able to stand up without falling back down and had to grab onto things for support. I wasn't hungry and was feeling almost too weak to eat. I called my younger sister who lived about twenty minutes away, to bring me some medicine and applesauce, which was about all I could manage to eat, although I wasn't vomiting. I assumed this was just a bad virus and after a week I was able to drive myself back home. I rested a few days more at home and then tried to resume normal activities, but found I was not up to doing much.

Our town had its end of summer block party and our

church participates in it, along with the local Rotary Club. I went to the event prepared to help out with our tag and food sales, but wound up leaving earlier than planned. After all the swimming, I should have had increased energy but the opposite was happening. Within two weeks I was sick again and shaking with chills worse than before. I didn't have the head pain this time but I noticed I was slowly losing strength in my legs and arms. I was taking over the counter medicine for cold and flu, plus ibuprofen for the pain, but nothing seemed to be of any help. I had to use a walker because it was becoming too painful to get up out of bed and my arms shook while I held onto it. My friend asked if I was going to the doctor and explained I had already called and there were no appointments available. Once again I found myself praying for enough strength to get to the toilet on time and or get off of it when I was done. I knew I probably should go to the hospital but I kept waiting to see if it would just run its course and I would be fine.

Then God answered me in a vision with a clear message. He used one of my favorite actors, Martin Sheen, in a scene from the *West Wing* series. There we were in the big office with some of the staff and in Sheen's voice, He said, "***I want a minute with my daughter***", as the staff was exiting the room. Then all I heard was a booming command of "**Go!**" I knew I had to get to the hospital.

I probably made a mistake in not going right away. This

is a relatively small town with a little over two thousand people in it, so it's not like living in the city where everything is within reach. People don't live so close they can pop over and take care of things at a moments notice. It made sense to me that I would need to first find some help to take care of my scardy-cat if I was not able to come right home, also I needed to pack a hospital bag, which in my condition was an all night project. So I waited until the next morning and then called an ambulance. It took four people to help me up and onto a stretcher. By the time I arrived at the hospital I was so weak, all I could do was lay there while they ran some tests and gave me fluids.

I was there quite a while and I could hear the hospital staff talking in the outer rooms and they seemed to be arguing about something. I needed to use the rest room and it took a while before I could get someone's attention. Finally a nurse or attendant came in and I asked for a walker to help get me to the bathroom. She brought it in and walked out again. I called for her to wait because I needed help but she didn't hear. I was up on a hospital bed and I could barely move without help. No one could hear me because they were bickering outside, so I started to sit up and work at lowering myself to where I could grab the walker. By that time I was in tears with the pain and I inched my way all the way to the bathroom, which fortunately had railings to hold me up as I did what I had to do and started back to the room. This bathroom trip took half an hour. I was sweating all over and crying and nobody seemed to notice as they were still complaining to each other about each other.

I was exhausted and feeling pretty much ignored and alone when all of a sudden my Pastor walked in the door. How did she even know I was there? Well, the thing about a small town is that when the siren goes off to signal fire or ambulance, there's always someone who's a volunteer, a relative, or a neighbor in those departments and the word gets around. Someone from our Church heard the siren and the address call and told my Pastor who happens to minister at the hospital on Thursday's, but this was a Friday and she "happened" to be covering for someone else's shift. It made me feel better to have someone there with me and I knew it had to be the Lord's handiwork that sent her. The timing was perfect because there was a battle coming and I needed support.

I could hear the doctor outside the room asking someone how I was doing. It didn't sound like the person who brought me the walker but they said, "well, she got up and went to the bathroom" Shortly after, the doctor who initially checked me in came into the room and told me they were not going to admit me and I could go home now. Did I hear right, was I hallucinating? Did he say, they weren't admitting me and go home? "The reason is" he said pointing to the paperwork, "failure to ambulate is not grounds for admittance". That meant even though I could not walk, it wasn't enough reason to be admitted. I was trying to process what he was telling me, but it just did not compute in my head, when he asked me, "so, how will you get home?" They carried me in, were they going to carry me home? I told him I was in no condition to go home.

Then I remembered what I heard the attendant say and explained to him that I did not just "get up and go" to the bathroom. I called for help and it took me over half an hour as I sweated and cried through the pain the whole way. Did he not understand this? Then he said he would send in the person from discharge to discuss options. She was a very nice young woman who explained why the doctor believed I was able to go home and also let me explain why I did not believe I could. She looked at me intently and slowly said, "You can refuse to be released and admit yourself". "Although you would be responsible for the hospital bills if you chose to self admit." She told me to think about it and she would return soon for my decision.

When she left I immediately turned to God and prayed about what to do. Clear as a bell I heard in my spirit "Stay". I felt such great relief to know the Lord was there with me and even as I am typing these words, I'm remembering that day with tears in my eyes. As if hearing from Him was not proof enough, what happened next could only be the grace of God. The woman returned with a doctor from the next shift. He was smiling and said not to worry, he looked over my chart and concluded I should absolutely be admitted, he had reversed the discharge order and told me coverage was approved for the stay. What a huge relief that was. I truly believe if I had been quick to obey the Lord on the day told me to *go*, then I wouldn't have been caught in the middle of the staff arguing between themselves and letting it affect their treatment of their patients.

This new doctor admitted me after seeing that I had a very elevated SED rate (rate at which red blood cells settle over time) and ran many other blood tests to find what was causing this inflammation throughout my body. There were at least four other doctors looking over my case testing and ruling out diseases, I was put on medication for fibromyalgia. Even though I did not have most of those symptoms, the medication for it was helping somewhat.

At the end of eight days they had done all they could for me without being further diagnosed by specialist outside the hospital. I was still not able to walk on my own or enough that I could take care of myself or climb the steps of my home. From the hospital I was transferred to a rehabilitation facility, where I spent another eight days, until I was able to manage going up steps one at a time.

During my stay at the hospital my Pastor was with me when I was first brought to my own room and we had a chance to speak with the doctor who admitted me. This opened the door for the doctor to mention he was a man of faith and later we had very good conversations about prayer and healing and how God works things out for those who believe in Him. At one point he mentioned I had a really positive attitude with all that was going on and that was an important part of getting well. I told him a much abbreviated version of my story and serving the Lord and I remembered I had my poetry and concept drawing with me. He also liked poetry and asked to make a copy to keep which made me happy.

In both the hospital and the rehab facility I met many people who were very open about sharing their faith and that was refreshing and uplifting, I felt surrounded by God's love and grace. One of the ministers who visited me asked to share my *Sing a New Psalm* poem with her daughter who is an artist, and then she came back to show me one of her paintings. It was of white birch trees overlaid with an open hand offering tree leaves in its palm. It was lovely. I have three people in my family who paint and draw beautifully and I tried for more than a year to get one of them to draw my tree concept but not one was available in all that time. Then here in the hospital someone walks in with a painting themed with what I envisioned. Was this a coincidence or part of God's plan? We exchanged information with the possibility of working together when I was feeling better.

After this I had another vision. Even with the new medication plus pain meds, I was having difficulty gaining strength but I did therapy everyday and showed improvement. I wondered if I was always going to need a walker or a cane. The plans I was imagining, for example a Christian youth center and camp, would require me to be more mobile. Then I had a vision of myself in the hospital hallway. *I was walking down the long corridor toward the light up ahead and I could see many birds gathering under a shelter of some type to my left side. As I walked past them I realized what was happening to me and said, "Hey! I'm walking and there's no pain!"* When I woke from it I knew I would be healed in this lifetime. Maybe you're thinking how do you know it wasn't "that big light in the sky"? I can only describe it by saying; these visions come with a sense of meaning in your spirit along with the image your mind is seeing. I believe the birds gathering in this vision represented a change in season and after I pass that season I will realize my healing.

In Christ we are *already* healed and restored and that is how God sees us. Some of us experience immediate healing, but for one reason or another the Lord brings us through a healing process and we just need to believe and trust His timing. There was hope, which helped me get through even more hospital time in the near future. I did do a follow up with a specialist but he had nothing to add or recommend for my condition and left me on the exact same medication.

By mid October I was able to go home and I took things very slowly. My poor cat was hiding from me for several hours before she came out from under the bed and hissed at me. She had never been separated from me for more than a day. She's rarely around other people and runs when anyone comes near just like a scardy-cat. I thought about her over those sixteen days probably meowing all around searching for me, hiding from my neighbor who fed her and I felt terrible about it. That night I prayed in Jesus' name, that if I should happen to die before my kitty does, would He please take us both at the same time because she would most likely be depressed or stressed to be without me. I know many people who think asking the Lord about such things is trivial or very selfish. In a way, since He has already given us His most precious only Son, anything we ask could be seen as trivial to God.

But God is merciful, loving and wants to pour out blessings on us, as we keep Him first in our lives. He cares about every detail of our lives.

In answering my prayer, He showed me a huge basket filled with all cat treats, toys and flowing lavender ribbons. Lavender is the package color of Trixie's absolute favorite milk flavored treats. Not only that, but soon after my cat began to let other people come near to pet her, feed and even brush her, which my family can testify never happened in the previous seven or eight years. To ask the Lord for something just for me used to be difficult, but He taught me through His Word and through other people, that this was a good thing to do. Not in a greedy way, but a thankful way, appreciating His presence before His presents.

*Up to this time you have not asked a [single] thing in
My Name [as]presenting all that I Am]; but now
ask and keep on asking and you will receive, so that
your joy (gladness, delight) may be full and complete.
John 16:24 (AMPC)*

When my sisters and I were very young, our dad drove us from our house in New York all the way to Pittsburg Pennsylvania to spend Christmas with his sister and her family. That's about a seven hour drive with three small children who were not allowed to make any noise during the trip. This was a man who had pulled the car over, made my sister get out of the car and pull her pants down so he could spank her severely on the side of the road. So we were as quiet as we could be and by the time we arrived at our aunt's house it was around dinnertime.

Like any kids being cooped up in the car, we were excited to run out, see our cousins and open presents. When they opened the door we said our hellos and asked, "Can we see our presents now?" I don't remember anything about that trip other than our dad beating us and beating into us, *never ever ask for anything from anyone and never expect a gift*. I didn't realize how much that one day affected certain situations throughout my life. If I went anywhere and couldn't pay my own way, I didn't go. I wasn't the girl who wanted a boyfriend just so she'd have a Valentine's Day gift. I was the extreme opposite and made sure I was alone so nobody had to waste money on a present for me, and that's just plain crazy.

While I certainly believe it's better to give than to receive, there are times that call for us to receive from others because it will benefit them as well. We all want to feel needed and that we have worth, so by receiving what someone gives us, whether it's a gift or some kind of help, we are letting them know they matter to us as we do to them.

The Lord put me in, or rather allowed me to be in different situations where I had to rely on others and ask for help. For example being in a hospital and having to ask for assistance in the bathroom because I simply could not help myself. It seems kind of funny that I would have no problem in helping someone in that situation, yet I found it a very humbling experience to need and ask for help. There were a number of times in other situations throughout my hospital stays, where I remember people using the specific words, "It's ok to ask for help". This was confirmation that whatever we want to give, whether that's love or help, spiritual or tangible, we also need to learn to receive those things to be usable by God. Now I understand that no matter what concerns or interests me, God is waiting to hear about it all, big or small.

Back at home and settled in I continued to work on creating my website and writing more poetry. I knew I would need not only a web-mailbox but a physical post office box where people could send copies of their art or poems as an option. I couldn't afford much so I went with a dollar figure in mind for the small P.O. Box. In keeping with the theme, I asked if certain numbers were available, according to some of my favorite Psalms. I asked at least a half dozen numbers and none were available. Then I asked, "Oh, what about 116?" The clerk said yes, it's available but it's a larger size. I knew it would cost too much but she quoted a lesser price. When I asked about the lower price she said, "It can be rented six months at a time". I didn't know that, so now I had a larger mailbox at a better price.

When I got home and went to check that off my to-do list for the website, I saw a note I had written nearly two years before which was, *P.O. Box 116?* I had completely forgotten about that and I started to laugh, then I heard in my spirit, "**This is a sign unto you, I am with you**". There is nothing in the world to compare with hearing the voice of God, and knowing He cares so greatly for us. I don't know if I could even write a description of how miraculous it is that this occurs, and to ordinary people.

There are no coincidences, only our Heavenly Father at work in our lives. One of my favorite movies to watch over and over is M. Knight Shyamalan's 'Signs'. It has to do with the possibility of an alien attack on Earth. Mel

Gibson plays a priest who lost his faith because he lost his wife to a seemingly coincidental accident. By the end of the movie we see his faith return by seeing the non-coincidental signs around him, some of which were spoken by God through his wife just before she passed away. For me this was not about whether or not aliens exist, but rather whatever may come against us, in all things God is with us.

After setting up the P.O. Box and also the web email address, it was getting into the fall holidays, so my time was split between working on the website, holiday shopping, cooking, Church events and visiting people.

On Christmas Eve, our little Church hosted the candlelight service so we were packed full. I was sitting in the back where I could stretch my legs and not trip anyone. In a certain portion of the service we stop and share the blessing of passing God's peace though handshaking and hugs. Unfortunately it was also cold and flu season and along with the peace, I got a piece of somebody's cold germs. I tried to escape a woman who kept sneezing and even used the Church hand sanitizer, but by the end of Christmas Day I was shivering under many blankets. This time around I was happy there wasn't much mucous because my lungs have a hard time expelling it, but I wasn't able to take a deep breath. Even with my inhaler, oxygen and cold medicine I seemed to be getting worse and my arms and legs hurt very much and had no strength. By New Year's Day, the prescription the hospital had given me wasn't working anymore.

When my friend called and firmly suggested I get to the hospital, I called my doctor, who called an ambulance, so I wouldn't have a repeat of the admittance incident. It was a busy day in the hospital as you might imagine during the Holiday season, but they took me right into get X-rayed and found I had pneumonia. I never knew a person could get pneumonia in so many ways, but you can get it from a virus, bacteria or fungus and of course from an infected person sneezing on you. They were admitting me right away, mainly due to the pneumonia, plus my SED rate was really high.

The woman doctor in charge of my case put me in a wheelchair while waiting for my room to be ready, so I thought it would be soon. With the pain in my arms and legs, it felt better to sit up and breathing was a little easier too. A couple of hours later the doctor came back and said the room was still not ready and she apologized that she had been called away from my case several times with other emergencies. I was praying for all those people and also to have a room soon, because I was really exhausted. I could hear all the commotion outside and waited patiently. We can't control the stuff that happens, only how we react to it, so better to deal with it calmly and patiently otherwise you're adding fuel to the fire.

However, as the eighth hour approached and I was still sitting in that wheelchair, I felt as if I might pass out from either the pain or dehydration. I didn't have much appetite and the only thing I had in the last day was medication with a little water. It was close to midnight when I got someone's attention and they brought a juice cup and a half sandwich. It took every bit of strength to open the seal of the juice cup and just after I drank it, the doctor came in with another person and the wheeled me to my room.

By that time I was so weak I couldn't stand at all and they called for extra help to get me to my feet, steady me and kind of lean me into the bed. I remember just wanting to sleep but they were asking questions, taking vitals, poking needles, hooking the fluid bags. I felt like E.T. after they found him by the river. Next thing I knew someone woke me at 5:00am and took more blood. Then the nurse came in and told me they were *flushing* my system with antibiotics. After I had some food in me I understood why she phrased it that way.

Finally the doctor in charge of my case came to explain things to me. She said she had come in to see me during the night but didn't have the heart to wake me, so she spent time studying my test results from last time, this time and the type of pain and inflammation I was having and compared that with other cases that presented similar symptoms. She actually had a name for it which was Polymyalgic Rheumatica. Having pneumonia triggered it to worsen. She changed the dosage of my medication, added a new one and within three days I was up and walking around.

I was home in less than a week and feeling good. The amazing part was that this particular Doctor had only been in that department for two weeks, and was supposed to be working somewhere else. Now a pessimistic non believer might think, so what good is going to church if God still gives you pneumonia, disease, and sends you to the hospital? But my joy is in the Lord who is always with me and knowing God works all things out for the good of those who love Him. The Lord is our Healer and is *never the cause* of any illness.

Anything bad comes from the evil one and in this life we all will have trials and tribulations. God allowed the pneumonia because He had gone before me, setting things in motion and working through this doctor to help me heal. It may sound coincidental, but really, how many coincidences do we need to experience before we believe it's a part of God's plan. God is alive, knows everywhere we go everything we do and is with us.

There's an idea from back in 1929 which became a pretty well known game after it was applied to an actor named Kevin Bacon, called *six degrees of separation*. Basically it states that any two people in the universe can be connected by at most five other acquaintances. Some other brainy people through the years believed it could be three degrees. I beg to differ with them all. I see the world as divided into only two groups which are those who believe in Christ and those who do not. Believers are said to be "in Christ" as He is in them. Therefore no degrees of separation can exist between those in Christ. All others are one degree away from knowing someone in Christ.

For I am persuaded beyond doubt (am sure) that neither death nor life, nor angels nor principalities, nor things impending and threatening nor things to come, nor powers,

Nor height nor depth, nor anything else in all creation will be able to separate us from the love of God which is in Christ Jesus our Lord.

Romans 8:38-39 (AMPC)

Finally I could move around and take short walks without experiencing pain with every step, which made doing daily chores mush easier. Although it was now the middle of winter and not many days warm enough to be outside, but at least I was better able to exercise indoors. On the plus side of winter, I had time for working on the website and writing poetry and researching some ideas for the future.

When the weather started to get warmer, which around here is only late April or May, I was able to walk around the yard for exercise and do simple yard work like putting bags of much around to keep weeds away. One day I was headed outside to go shopping. My car was in the garage about fifty feet from the house and from my front door I need to go about six feet and then down seven steps. This particular Spring-like day I prayed as always when I went out, which is usually from *Psalm 91* or *Psalm 23*. In the middle of praying as I put my foot out onto the first step I heard "CRACK!", and the stairs collapsed under me, leaving me facedown and twisted between wood, concrete and mulch. I stayed still and processed what just happened and feeling pain in my legs, knee and arm. I didn't hit my head but the rest of me was in-between the steps and at first I couldn't move any which way to get loose from them. There's virtually no traffic on my road and you might see ten to fifteen cars on a busy day. One car passed but didn't see me. I slowly managed to move some wood enough to inch my way out of the pile and sit up. I could see my right knee and leg starting to swell and my let arm had a huge bruise where it hit the wood and a nail ripped some skin so I was bleeding.

After my last trip to the hospital I still had not developed enough strength to get up from a sitting on the ground position and now I was in real pain. Another car passed and just kept going. Then one of the towns road crew trucks backed into my neighbor's driveway directly across the road from me. I thought surely he was maneuvering to come over and help me. I was waving my cane at him as he pulled out of the driveway and turned the other direction. I was sitting there wondering, how in the world did he miss seeing me? I thought, "God I know you're going to get me out of this but why didn't they see me?" Then I remembered my cell phone and looked for anyone who could get here. I called a few people but only reached voicemail.

So as I was sitting there I felt like crying but instead I laughed because I remembered Joyce Meyer, telling a story that fit this situation. It went something like, *a woman was in a boat and while praying, for some reason the boat tipped or flipped sending her into the water. She came to the surface and asked God, "How could you let that happen to me even while I was praying?" God replied. "You're still alive aren't you?* So I said, "OK Lord, thank-you, I know it could have been worse, so please help me get up and get help."

It probably would have been much worse if I hadn't just put mulch down two days before. Was that a Coincidence? I think not! I could see a big plastic bucket with rope handles under the deck. I was able to hook the handle with my cane, bring it over, flip it and lean on it until I could straighten my legs enough to get up. I had no front steps to get in the house, so I leaned against the house and slowly walk around back and up three steps to get inside. Finally I got hold of a friend from Church who brought me to the hospital. She waited with me the whole time which was several hours while they X-rayed me and gave me a shot for tetanus etc...

I had that same doctor who did not want to admit me

on a previous occasion but I had already forgiven him for that and he was very pleasant this time. Nothing was broken but I had severe contusions to the leg and that was pretty ouchy for quite a long time. Being off my feet recovering gave me time to launch the website on Father's Day. With that set in motion, I thought I finally had done something for the Lord, by making a place on the web where we can creatively worship Him by sharing our gifts in praise. Once the website caught on, I knew it would enable me to raise funds and start a Christian based non-profit and then finally I would have something to write about!

14- UNCOMMON BLESSING & FINAL EXAM

So now finish doing it, that your [enthusiastic] readiness in desiring it may be equaled by your completion of it according to your ability and means. 2 Corinthians 8:11 (AMPC)

I have strength for all things in Christ Who empowers me [I am ready for anything and equal to anything through Him Who infuses inner strength into me; I am self-sufficient in Christ's sufficiency]. Philippians 4:13 (AMPC)

When our earthly journey is over and judgment day is here, each one of us will stand before God and give an account of our lives.

It's not about our sins which were already judged at the Crucifixion of Christ, but what good did we do with our lives, while we had opportunity and unlimited resources through the risen Christ our Lord. On our way to Omega, every new day brings a plethora of opportunities to do something good for someone else, having no earthly expectation of compensation or reward.

Blessed and happy and to be envied are those whose iniquities are forgiven and whose sins are covered up and completely buried. Blessed and happy and to be envied is the person of whose sin the Lord will take no account nor reckon it against him. Romans 4:7-8 (AMPC)

If we believe in our hearts, Christ is our Lord and Savior; we will go to Heaven even if we haven't done much else. Some people only learn the Truth in their hearts shortly before they die and they too are forgiven and saved. It almost seems unfair that some can be so blessed at the last minute. But what if you were that someone in need of God's miraculous Love? The Lord gives us the parable of *the workers in the vineyard*, who all received equal pay for unequal work.

But he answered one of them, 'I am not being unfair to you, friend. Didn't you agree to work for a denarius? Take your pay and go. I want to give the one who was hired last the same as I gave you. Don't I have the right to do what I want with my own money? Or are you

envious because I am generous?' Matthew 20:13-15 (AMPC)

As for those of us who grow our faith daily by reading and hearing the Word of God, we are being transformed in our hearts, our minds and our spirits. We get to a place where *our cup runneth over* (Psalm 23) and we feel a need to share our blessings with others in whatever form that takes, but it's usually both tangible and spiritual.

Now may the God Who gives the power of patient endurance (steadfastness) and Who supplies encouragement, grant you to live in such mutual harmony and such full sympathy with one another, in accord with Christ Jesus, That together you may [unanimously] with united hearts and one voice, praise and glorify the God and Father of our Lord Jesus Christ (the Messiah). Romans 15:5-6 (AMPC)

Creating a devotional website was only one way for me to share my love for the Lord. Together with the other contributors to the website, we share an opportunity to bring hope and help to those in need. I knew it had a place in God's plan for me because of certain things He told me. One of those things was to be patient. Without funds to advertise the site there wasn't much response. I knew it would take some time before I could upgrade it professionally, so all I could do was wait patiently. In the meantime I began to organize my notes on what I would eventually about write in my book, including all of the dreams and things the Lord had been teaching me.

That summer like every year, there was a back to school mega-sale with note books, pens, and all kinds of supplies. I purchased about twenty spiral notebooks two dozen pens, and many pads of note paper. In one note book I wrote all the ideas I had for the non-profit organization and all the things that might grow from it.

I remember one of the mailings I got from Joyce Meyer's Ministries about a particular mission she was planning over seas and it really touched my heart. I prayed for my website to be on its way so I would soon be able to contribute more to missions of that kind. I thought about my current circumstances which was a lack of funds and semi-ok physical health, and I just felt tears welling up in my eyes. Then I heard as if He was sitting next to me whispering, "***Be not uneasy child, your time has not come yet to shine***". So I let the tears fall because this was a good kind of crying. The great love and timing of our God, is always perfect, coming just when we need to feel His presence. It's an almost indescribable feeling of peace to know God is willing to be as close with us now, as Jesus was with the Apostles all those years ago.

It was soon after when I had another vision. In it, I saw myself pregnant and it seemed to me, this would be my second child. I've *never* had such a dream before so this was kind of shocking, especially since I have no children and have never been pregnant. Unless there would be a new miracle birth to write about, I figured it had to be some kind of message. But what was the message? Once again God's timing cleared things up for me. I was watching one of Joyce's sermons about, no longer being baby Christians and being able to do something with what we've learned. I'm not quoting here but, she spoke about this as being pregnant with knowledge or an idea, and after it forms we will give birth to a project or something to that effect. Wow, at least now I had an idea of what that vision meant. I figured the website must be this second pregnancy and birth and there were certainly some labor pains involved. Hmm...then I wondered was the website my first child, and now there's another one on the way? I really couldn't put this puzzle together. Whether it was the first or second, it seemed I had a missing bundle of joy to find!

My mind was convinced there needed to be external evidence, like a successful website or a non-profit organization started, as proof before I could write about how God was working in my life. Looking over at my pile of notebooks and collected scraps of paper where I scribbled my visions, I began to copy them into a notebook. Sitting with all my writing tools I looked at that pile as if it was the complete story of my life and I was waiting for the successful ending so I could begin writing. Then the Lord said to me, "**Stop This Procrastination**", along with a few other things about my writing. Things went through my mind like, "What?

Was I doing that? What should I be doing?" Then it dawned on me, my first child was this book! It seemed like the idea of it had been in my head for so long but I was focusing on being successful at doing something for the Lord. My real story is not about anything I could possibly do for God, but rather what God has already done for me. The procrastination messages kept coming. It seemed every sermon, email, video or radio show mentioned procrastination, procrastination, procrastination. So I said, "OK Lord, I got it now, but please help me if I get stuck and help me to write a good and true testimony".

I know God loves me and gave His only Son for me to be offered as a sacrifice, taking the punishment I deserved for my sins. When Jesus Christ was resurrected from the dead, He went back to the Father, but proposed an invitation to be in His wedding ceremony. In my case, I humbly accepted, so He sent the Holy Spirit to help me get ready for Revelation of that day. If that sounds a bit presumptuous or personal, that's because it's *very* personal. God not only gave me the gift of life, but when I made a mess of it and tried to end it, He saved me and gave me a new life.

That intimate bond is eternal and so is God's love. But of course, it's not just for me; it's for whosoever believes that Christ is their Lord and Savior. I know there are many people who grew up believing some of the same things as I did about Christianity. They're walking around feeling guilty about something and avoid going to church or conversations about religion, because they were taught about old rules but not the precious new relationship. Before I was reborn I never met anyone who talked about the Lord communicating to them in the ways I've described in this book. The Lord knew my heart, so He kept bringing those people and things into my life, until I understood that He was with me the whole time and waiting for me to acknowledge His presence.

Since being reborn I've met others who hear His voice and it's so very apparent because they're joyful people and eager to talk about how He's working in their lives. It's called the good news for a reason!

There is a whole new crop of born-again-Christians out there who are sharing the Word of God through their music, movies, books, and websites, in their schools, Churches and neighborhoods. They understand the active power of speaking God's Word. They are helping, healing and saving people both spiritually and physically, both figuratively and literally. God is love and we are forgiven. All He asks of us is to believe that, love Him and love others.

He will take care of all we need. As I mentioned at the beginning of this book, I thought I was happy in spite of some unhappy incidents. So if someone like me was willing to give up on life, what chance of hope or help is out there for those who have been through worse or suffered much more than me?

We live in a world which seems to be in its last days. We are witnessing daily acts of barbarism and persecution. There's terrorism in every country. People die of hunger every minute of every day. Disaster is a constant news feature. Not only that but it's as if there's a new wave of racism sweeping over us and segregation of people into categories with different rights. There is an increase in malevolent behavior and callousness toward people and even animals. What are we supposed to do about any of it?

What better time could there be to know we are children of God and have His peace, protection and the power of His Word?

And God's peace [shall be yours, that tranquil state of a soul assured of its salvation through Christ, and so fearing nothing from God and being content with its earthly lot of whatever sort that is, that peace] which transcends all understanding shall garrison and mount guard over your hearts and minds in Christ Jesus. Philippians 4:7 (AMPC)

Since we are living in the end times, our only true hope is in Jesus. I pray that the Church would keep the focus on the New Testament and Jesus Christ. The Church can not be built up with the old way of what we shall not do and throwing stones at sinners, but it can be built up with what we shall do, as we are made righteous in Christ. All things are possible with God as we live in Christ, acknowledging true wisdom which comes via the Holy Spirit.

I found that when I first tried to do things the right way on my own, the devil would come at me by putting unwanted or malicious thoughts in my mind and reminding me of past failures. Satan roams around trying to destroy and tear down every good thing. He can't read our thoughts but his attack starts in our minds. He'll throw misleading, negative, hateful or vengeful thoughts at us, hoping they will stick inside and grow like malignant tumors. He wants us to react badly or fear that God will reject us. Whenever I began to pray, open my Bible or sometimes even think about Jesus, a very nasty word would be right there in my thoughts. I kept asking the Lord for forgiveness because that's not really how I thought at all and I didn't understand why that was happening. It was pretty unnerving to know that evil could get in my head against my will.

Then I heard several different preachers explaining they had the same kind of experience as they began to following Christ. It's Satan's purpose to destroy us and he patiently waits for opportunities to defeat our progress toward knowing God's love and good plan for our lives. The Lord already knows those things are not coming from us and meditating on His Word will help clarify and strengthen our minds.

As believers we are joint-heirs with Christ, we claim the benefit of having the mind of Christ and can do all things in His strength. We have the ability to discard negative thoughts that pop into our head. Now I've learned when I want to discard a thought or behavior; I need to replace it with a better thought or better behavior. Something good needs to fill that void or it will remain open for another attack. For example when you make a mistake, if you want to stop saying "I am so stupid! What was I thinking?" replace the old negative words with the new positive words that begin with the same letter or words that sound similar. It takes getting used to it, but soon you'll be saying, "I am not stupid, I am becoming stupendous and I have the mind of Christ!" We can call that, Christian replacement therapy. Satan wants to grab hold of you if he can, but he'll move on to an easier target if hears you speaking the Word of God. The devil didn't want me meditating on or saying the name of Jesus, because then he would have to leave the premises. Enough talk about the evil one and back to the love of God.

Keeping God first in my life has given me a way to have peace in my life no matter what goes on around me or in the world. I don't mean to suggest ignoring important issues, but only that it's comforting to know God is faithful to keep His promises and nothing can separate me from His love. At any given moment my circumstances can change for better or worse, but God's love for me does not change and I can trust and rely on Him, to be with me in troubled times and in joyful times.

I find myself laughing at some of the simple ways He blesses me. Our Church started a local food pantry and each year the pantry fills special holiday baskets for Thanksgiving and Christmas. Each local Church or business donates one particular item, but enough to fill around one hundred & twenty-five baskets. Our item was turkey gravy. I look for sales on everything all year long, yes; I am a bargain-hunter-holic. Around September, I asked to Lord to go shopping with me and find some bargains. I was in a well known department store that carries a little bit of everything. On my way to the food side of the store, there were fixtures on wheels, stacked with newly marked down items. I made a mental note to look there on the way out, but, as I got closer I saw jars that looked like gravy. Sure enough they were turkey gravy and the price was twenty-five cents each! If you have ever bought gravy in a jar, you know it can cost ten times that much. These were three cases of name brand gravy for a quarter per jar. How convenient for me, yippee! I think I left a few jars because I didn't want to be greedy, but it was after all, for a good cause. That's why I never go shopping without the Lord.

Another beautiful thing the Lord did for me, was to plant two evergreen trees. I love the smell of pine trees and love all evergreens. There are lots of them up here in the mountains, but not on my property. When I moved in there was one huge evergreen right in front of my house. There were also three tiny skinny trees trying to grow but they were in a crowded space and getting no sunlight. During my second year here, Simon Strange asked if I had anything for him to do around the yard. So he wound up replanting one of the wimpy trees in a central spot a few yards from a stream, where it could eventually grow and be seen from the driveway as my Christmas tree. Unfortunately in less than three months it died and shriveled up. I pulled it up and trashed it with other lawn debris. It was a few years after that; Simon didn't come to visit anymore.

Another year later in springtime, I noticed an evergreen growing on the opposite side of the little stream which runs across my property and also straight back from the driveway. It was growing right by the water's edge in more perfect spot than I could have picked, where it wouldn't block the view of the flowing water when it grew. I knew after hearing a sermon on this scripture, the Lord planted it for just me as a sign to show He was with me and cared even about such little things. That tree grew faster than any other tree here. It's taller and fuller than the *much older* scrawny trees which are still here to remind me of how much I have grown since being replanted in Christ.

And he shall be like a tree firmly planted [and tended] by the streams of water, ready to bring forth its fruit in

its season; its leaf also shall not fade or wither; and everything he does shall prosper [and come to maturity]. Psalm 1:3 (AMPC)

When I realized the tree could be seen from anywhere outside, but I couldn't actually see the tree from my living room window, I was a *tiny* bit sad. The next year, in Spring I looked out the living room window to see there was a second tree growing in a perfect spot for viewing and I just had to laugh. He knows our hearts desires down to the slightest details. As we live each day leaning on the Lord, we change and things in our life start to change for the better. It seems as though the Lord is always doing little things to make my life easier, giving me the freedom to reach out and be helpful to others. Some may regard these things as trivial nonsense, but the Lord wastes no opportunity to bless those who believe in Him.

For years I had trouble just getting a simple prescription to be correctly filled and covered by insurance. Between the doctor, the pharmacy and the insurer, something always went wrong and I'd spend hours on the phone to straighten out the mess only to be frustrated when it happened again the very next time. As I kept believing in God's goodness and favor toward us, I lifted even these little type of problems to the Lord and soon everyone seemed to be in sync.

When there was a mix up after office hours and they couldn't fill my prescription, the pharmacist gave me a free sample of the medicine until the issue could be resolved, which it was and hasn't happened since.

I called my satellite company over a data issue, and they gave me a nice size credit and a per month discount without me asking for anything. My bank has waved certain fees, and my utility company told me my account was protected when there were some strange issues going on with my bill. This kind of good stuff never happened to me before!

Then there was an incident with my car which can not just be coincidence. The main highway near me is two lanes each direction with nice long entrances and exits. You can drive for miles with no cars in sight but in a rush hour you might see eight or ten. Recently I was on my way home and had a mixed CD playing. There was no traffic so I was using cruise control. As I got closer to home the song playing was that one about, Jesus taking the wheel. At the exact moment I approached the exit I was singing along to the first line of the chorus and *before* I could move my foot to hit the brake it shifted out of cruise control and slowed itself down at the exit ramp. I think the Lord took the wheel just for fun. It never happened again since, but I know it wasn't a glitch in the system.

When we believe, rely and trust in the Lord, even though we will still face challenges, if we keep on believing, we'll start seeing good results and blessings surrounding us.

My younger sister and her husband have two sons. My older nephew needed his passport and identification card for something but couldn't find them. My sister mentioned it to me and I told her I would pray for it to be found. Sadly they all kept looking for a period of three months and never found them. They live in another state so I rarely get to visit, but when I had the opportunity I drove down.

When I got there I said my hellos to my sister and younger nephew. My older nephew was upstairs, so I went up briefly and said hello and headed back to the kitchen area. We were just catching up on little tidbits of news they way families do, when my sister mentioned they still hadn't found the passport. Exactly at that moment I saw a vision of two passports in my mind. I told her I must have seen them here, I just saw the picture in my mind so I must have passed them by somewhere. I explained the details of how I saw, 'Passport', stamped in gold on two large brown booklets. Also, I saw a spot-light from above focused on them, like one of those old crime movies, where the criminal is being questioned by a detective in a darkened room. She told me no, it was one dark blue passport with the I.D. card, and that I probably saw something the kids made in grade school for a project. I disagreed and said this looked pretty real to me, and it would be easy to retrace my steps since I hadn't been there very long. She said, "It's been three months and we've looked everywhere, but go ahead, take a look". I started in the kitchen wherever I had been, then the restroom, and then headed upstairs. I knocked on the door of my nephews room, and when he said come in, I opened it, explained what I was going to look for and stepped into the room. I took another step, turned to the left looking at a pile of papers and books on his desk and said, "I'll start right here, is this it?" His desk had a lamp and at the base I saw the blue passport with the I.D. card sticking out from it. He jumped up, "What?!" He explained how impossible that was, because they had searched every inch of the house. I said that is God's work and we hugged. When I went back downstairs, they didn't believe me especially since it happened so quickly. My other nephew ran up to see for himself.

With family it's sometimes harder for them to understand the person they've know their whole lives, is somehow becoming this new creature. It was hard enough for me to understand and I'm the living proof! I believe the Holy Spirit showed me the "brown" passports and also waited all those months until I was there in person for several reasons. I was adamant about the color, size and number of what I saw and I really thought I must have seen it and it didn't occur to me it was a vision until afterward. This was proof that what happened didn't come from me; it came *through* me from the Holy Spirit living in me. I *hadn't* actually seen the passport before I found it, or I would have known there was only one, which was small and blue with another card sticking out of it. If nobody could find it in all that time, but then it's found in such a strange way, the credit can only go to God at work in our lives.

You still need more proof? OK, here's more. Remember me mentioning how much easier it was to exercise in that pool? Well, other good stuff happened in that very same pool at another time.

I was enjoying the cool water on a really hot day and my cell phone rang at the side of the pool. It was a very close friend who had been going through one personal trauma after another until it seemed to affect every area of her life. She was overwhelmed and sobbing to the point where I almost couldn't understand her words. I could feel how much pain she was in and I knew if she were with me in person there was something I could do to help. Not that you can't help someone over the phone, but this particular person was someone dear to me and I knew the pressure of certain things was tearing the life right out of her. I was not able to drive to her, so she agreed to drive cautiously and come over for a visit.

Because we've known each other so long and so well, we could talk about anything together and were never judgmental, just there for each other. She was a Christian who went to catholic school and was taught all those things which either make us afraid of God, only able to pray in Church, wonder where He is, or turn away because we believe He let us down. There are far too many people without much hope of seeing God's love in their lives.

After we talked for a while about the problems she was facing, I reminded her of what the Lord was doing in my life and how much better I felt as I kept believing and learning to put my trust in Him. I could feel that she was at a crucial point in her life. Anything I suggested in the past might have helped for a little while but as humans, *on our own* there will always be a limit to our strength and abilities to help each other. This was the right opportunity for her to *let God be God* in her life, and stop struggling to do everything on her own. She agreed to accept and acknowledge Jesus as her Lord and Savior and ask for His help in her life. In the middle of the pool treading water, we held hands and prayed a very simple prayer of salvation, and the moment we finished, a beautiful butterfly landed on her shoulder. What a comforting sign! I had chills and it wasn't from the pool water. She couldn't quite see it on her shoulder so I carefully moved it by its wing to her arm where it stayed for some time before hopping over to me and then flying up and away. I knew that as I kept praying for her, God would work in her life as He did in mine.

He changes us little by little, renewing our health and strength, surrounding us with people who will help us to grow on our journey. He does so much more than we see or acknowledge, so at first it may seem to be something we've finally done right on our own. But the Lord's work won't be ignored, and He'll help us gain understanding and wisdom, and to realize there are no coincidences, just part of His plan for us.

My friend and I recently talked and she was telling me about how good everything was going with her family and her life. She was happy in her relationships, her job, and struggles of the past, didn't appear to be in her present! That was an answered prayer for me. It's painful for us when we see someone we love and care about, who's hurting in so many ways, but we can't seem to help them no matter what advice we give or how many ways we try. The Lord worked it out; He knows the way, because He *is* the Way.

We are assured and know that [God being a partner in their labor] all things work together and are [fitting into a plan] for good to and for those who love God and are called according to [His] design and purpose. Romans 8:28 (AMPC)

Well, I hope I have given you good things to think about. God loves you and wants to be part of your life, and that relationship is what our journey is all about. He has a great plan for your life, but you have to participate and you start by inviting Him into your life. He will never leave you struggling to do things on your own as you trust Him to make whatever changes need to be made.

He will always love you and bring hope to your heart. Be thankful for His mercy and grace, and He will lead you to a life of abundance and prosperity.

Now to Him Who, by (in consequence of) the [action of His] power that is at work within us, is able to [carry out His purpose and] do superabundantly, far over and above all that we [dare] ask or think [infinitely beyond our highest prayers, desires, thoughts, hopes, or dreams]— Ephesians 3:20 (AMPC)

If you're already a Christian and you haven't heard from the Lord personally yet, know that if you ask Him to speak to you, He will use whichever way is best for you. Watch for signs and accept the help He sends into your life. As you grow you'll get better at listening and hearing. However, if you want to make progress on your journey with the Lord, then let go of anything that holds you back from hearing, like fear, hate, jealousy, bitterness, condemnation and unforgiveness. With Christ you have the power to let go of the past and begin again. You can have joy in your life and peace in your heart.

See the world without compartments needlessly labeled by race, color, gender, social status, wealth, political party and other things which tend to divide people. When faced with situations that cause you to be confused, turn to Jesus. Know that Jesus never turned away from a person in need of His love and He did not judge them. He showed them mercy; spoke to them with patience and kindness, forgave them, healed them and freed them from the curse of sin.

For God did not send the Son into the world in order to judge (to reject, to condemn, to pass sentence on) the world, but that the world might find salvation and be made safe and sound through Him. John 3"17 (AMPC)

People are only saved and unsaved. Jesus saves and He is the answer to all we are searching for in life. He is the Truth the Life and the Way, and we all become one in Christ.

May the God of your hope so fill you with all joy and peace in believing [through the experience of your faith] that by the power of the Holy Spirit you may abound and be overflowing (bubbling over) with hope. Romans 15:13 (AMPC)

May you be blessed

On your way to

Omega

ON THE WAY TO OMEGA…

POEMS

Sing A New Psalm...

A seed from Your bounty was planted anew

with a measure of faith in my heart till it grew

strong roots took hold nourished by Almighty Love

and broke free from deep earth seeking light from above

branching out through every season

though many storms left their trace

this tree will eternally flourish

saved by Your Amazing Grace

the breeze carries Your voice

so gentle and calm

now every leaf unfolds for You

to sing a new psalm...

June Anne Abele

ON THE WAY TO OMEGA…

Thorn in My Pride

When I'm out in the world

Trying to reach a new height

Sidestepping Your direction

But not hidden from Your sight

When I've made the wrong selection

When I end up in a fight

When my stubbornness loathes correction

Convinced my wrong is right

Please let Your Holy Spirit

Help my anger to subside

Remind me of forgiveness

That Your arms are open wide

When I've hurt the ones You love

Help me quickly apologize

Remind me You still love me too

Please Jesus, be the thorn in my pride

JUNE ANNE ABELE

When everything around me

Warns to look out for myself

When distractions overtake me

And put Your Word upon a shelf

When my pursuit of happiness

Omits those who need my help

When I gamble for petty gain

Forgetting the hand that You were dealt

Let Your Holy Spirit

Dwell in me and be my guide

Convict me of my selfishness

In Your Word I will abide

Bring me to my knees in prayer

Like the soldier who pierced Your side

When I forget how much You love me

Jesus, be the thorn in my pride

June Anne Abele

ABOUT THE AUTHOR

June Anne Abele, is a born-again Christian, who's been led by the Holy Spirit through lots of growing pains in the last decades and is happy to share them if it will help someone else be healed. She lives in rural Upstate, NY, with her cat named Trixie and some great neighbors. She's thankful to God, for her love of music, poetry, all kinds of animals and the gift of nature which is the greatest show on Earth. She is blessed with two sisters and their families, who are all quirky, creative and very loved. June is looking forward to writing about some new adventures, as the Lord faithfully continues to direct her steps on the way to Omega. Update: During the writing of this book, the Holy Spirit led June, to volunteer at a local Christian based community thrift-shop. The opportunities to meet new people and help in tangible ways, with joy of heart, have already begun. It's clearly time to *Sing a New Psalm!*

www.ingramcontent.com/pod-product-compliance
Lightning Source LLC
LaVergne TN
LVHW091711070526
838199LV00050B/2355